WRITERS REPUBLIC

THE
FAULT
IN US

MARTA REINOSO

WRITERS REPUBLIC L.L.C.
515 Summit Ave. Unit R1
Union City, NJ 07087, USA

Website: *www.writersrepublic.com*
Hotline: *1-877-656-6838*
Email: *info@writersrepublic.com*

Ordering Information:
Quantity sales. Special discounts are available on quantity purchases by corporations, associations, and others. For details, contact the publisher at the address above.

Library of Congress Control Number:		IN-PROCESS
ISBN-13:	978-1-64620-654-4	[Paperback Edition]
	978-1-64620-655-1	[Digital Edition]

Rev. date: 12/03/2020

DEDICATION

♥

To my husband who is my #1, my best friend, moral support, inspiration, and my rock. Thank you baby for all that you do for us. Your family looks up to you and loves you very much!

"Your time is limited, so don't waste it living someone else's life. Don't be trapped by dogma – which is living with the results of other's opinions drown out your own inner voice. And most important, have the courage to follow your heart and intuition. They somehow already know what you truly want to become. Everything else is secondary." - Steve Jobs

"Love suffers long and is kind. It is not proud. Love bears all things, believes all things, hopes all things, and endures all things. Love never fails. And now these three remain: faith, hope and love. But the greatest of these is **Love**.*"* - Corinthians 13

PROLOGUE

"What? No way! I would never make you my agent if I become famous. You know how shitty celebrities treat their agents?" Lilly exclaims to Desmarie. Both Desmarie and Lilly, being as close as they are, always wondered what would happen if they became famous in the future. Would they travel around the world? Would they be rich? Would they still talk to each other, and maintain a strong relationship? As the discussion persisted, Desmarie looked up, smiled while exhaling and expressed how important Lilly was to her. She had stated that if Lilly was ever to become a famous celebrity, she should hire Desmarie herself to be her agent, that way they would be able to work together; an opportunity to remain close friends. When Lilly asserted a big NO toward Desmarie's question, they both smiled and just stayed quiet. "I can't believe I am leaving; it feels like I just moved in here," Desmarie mentioned while drinking her cup of coffee and packing her stuff. Lilly swallowed a big gulp of her ice pop and slowly reminisced, "Things are going to be so different with you gone."

CHAPTER 1

The Beginning

Born in Madrid, Spain, Desmarie always thought she had something fascinating to be able to express to herself and others around her. In this lifetime, society continued to grow daily, making the public eye more judgmental towards what someone looks like and what they do in this unhinged world we call earth.

Traveling back in time to the mid 90's, Desmarie lived in an apartment with her mother and 3 siblings. Residing in the sunshine state, where there were no seasonal changes of weather, except rain and humidity with sun. Desmarie spent her days going to grade school, then coming home and usually playing outside in her apartment complex with her friends. She was usually shy and not very social when it came to girls, but it was always easier to trail with the boys. As a tomboy herself, she had hobbies that included trading Pokémon cards, riding bikes, and going to malls with her sister Babi. "Hey is Desmarie home? I got new holographic cards, I know she would want to check these out!" a kid from the complex came by and stood in the front door, while Babi when to get her little sister. It was a hot day out, Desmarie's friend was pacing back and forth and kept looking at his Pokémon card until Desmarie finally came out. No way you got Machamp! Ugh but my holographic Hitmonchan is so pretty, not sure I want to give it up and trade," Desmarie looked down at her binder of cards with a worried look on her face, decided to keep her shiny original Hitmonchan. "That's ok, I going to trade more cards with my brother and see if you like any of those. See you later Desmarie!" Her friend runs off and heads to the stairs to go down to his apartment where he lived. Desmarie resided in a big apartment complex where she got along with most of her neighbors who were in her age group as well.

Maria, which is Desmarie's mother, had brought her family to this red, white and blue country from a connection of a close friend. Just like now, America is considered the land of opportunity and land of the free. As many immigrants, Desmarie's family came to this country to hopefully gain citizenship, stay to live and work permanently without any worries. Maria has been dealing with a lot, including a never-ending divorce process with the father of her kids. Cigarette after cigarette, she would feel ongoing stress that just wouldn't let up. She would spend her time and days at work, which was cleaning other peoples' houses, getting home super tired, making sure all of her 4 kids were good and taken care by every day. Desmarie, being the youngest, was usually taken care by Babi who was the middle sister and enjoyed very much helping her mother.

"Oh cool! Lunchables! I never get to have these!" Desmarie bursts out with happiness when she opens her lunchbox at school. Her classmates give a random look but goes along and smiles with Desmarie while eating their lunch in the cafeteria. Lunchables were valuable in Desmarie's household. They were usually one of the pricier items in the supermarket, and given their tight financial establishment at home with the family, this was a rare surprise to open up and eat.

As years pass, Maria continues to work her same maintenance job and the kids continue with their schooling. Starting to get a bit chilly at night, Miami in Florida usually had cold fronts that would last around 4-5 days. It felt nice, and all together it felt like Desmarie lived up north or somewhere in the middle of the country where seasons actually existed.

It is the month of November, Sunday night the 22nd and it was Maria's 46th birthday. Desmarie remembers how beautiful her mother looked, dressed in black, looking as stunning as any woman can appear to one's eyes. Having her life with her children beside her, that is all that mattered and that is all that she ever wanted. Although everything wasn't perfect, she felt accomplished to the set goals.

A knock followed during a day of celebration that night. One of Desmarie's sisters goes to open the door, and it was a tall, blue-eyed older man standing in front of them wearing a plaid button-down shirt with jeans and dress shoes. He greeted everyone, then walked up to Maria. "Hello, you must be Maria, my name is Victor and I know one of your daughters; Babi. She advised me that tonight was your birthday. I am sorry it's late in the hour but I wanted to make sure I introduce myself to you and wish you many blessings on this special occasion." Maria had a good feeling and felt romantically aghast. While staring into his eyes, she shook his hand showing a big grin on her face.

CHAPTER 2

Love at First Sight

Desmarie was too young to know what love was, but one thing she didn't really take to heart nor believed, was love at first sight. She remembered her mother looking at Victor with a mesmerizing glow. The vivid blue seeing in his twinkling eyes almost lost Maria in her path and surroundings, which eventually came to feel like she was floating in space. "Thank you very much, but you didn't have to come, you are too kind," Maria suggested after meeting Victor. She spoke with a heavy accent, but she knew most of the basics of the English language.

Beyond Desmarie's belief, the two hit it off quite nicely. Victor took Maria to the opera for her birthday as a gift. Desmarie was captivated and content, knowing her mother was having an amazing time with Victor. It was about time she began to enjoy herself, living her life and actually caring for herself for once; having a good time. Victor spent his days talking with her, spending time with her and going out to different restaurants and social events with her. Desmarie noticed her mother looking more and more happy, not as stressed and drained as she would normally act throughout the days, weeks and months. The smoking continued; it didn't help that Victor was a smoker as well. Shining a light on this topic, Victor noticed Maria's chronic cough and while realizing it for himself as well, he helped and guided for both to quit smoking.

As the year flew by with many changes happening, vivacity remained between Maria and Victor. He began to tell her how he ended up here in Miami and how he originally is from New Jersey. Victor would travel down to Florida every Winter and spend the season here to avoid the snow and all of the other work that came with maintaining the harsh weather conditions up north. Maria found everything about Victor so captivating and influential. Victor also took it upon himself to help them both stop a bad habit; smoking. Thinking deep down, Desmarie and her family wished someone like him would have come along a lot sooner than now; mom deserves all of the joy she can get. Too many years passed filled with worry and affliction. After time, what has come to realization to many was that hard work eventually pays off. Oh and of course, there is someone out there for everyone, including Desmarie's mother Maria who is finally where she wants to be in life. She was happy, safe, and excited to begin the upcoming days waking up next to Victor.

CHAPTER 3

The Move

It all happened so fast. Maria was head over heels in love with Victor. The two spent countless days together. Desmarie was starting grade school and has been making new friends along the way. It was an end to the school year, beginning the summer visiting New Jersey which was Victor's original state of residence.

As Maria's divorce finally came to be finalized, Victor without hesitation, proposed to her. Even though it felt so quick, Maria gave her hand in marriage on August 17th, 2000. She ended up moving up north with Victor to his home and began her new life with the love of her life. Her older children were happy for her, however, they ended up staying in Miami to continue their lives with school and their partners at the time. Desmarie, being the youngest, went with her mother and now step-father Victor to live in New Jersey.

Desmarie felt a little bit nervous about the new move, but happy and couldn't complain since she still gets to be with her mother, who was always her life. Desmarie didn't spend much time with her siblings, although there through thick and thin, the sibling bond wasn't big due to the age difference. As Desmarie was the youngest, following 9 years after her brother, hang-outs were usually with mom and Victor. Both her sisters and brother would spend most of their time with their friends. This move wasn't at all stressful and anyways, for a 10-year-old it was a piece of cake.

Desmarie wakes up to the smell of bacon and eggs in the morning. Victor's house, which was technically now both Maria and Desmarie's home as well, was very cozy and undoubtedly bigger and more spacious compared to the apartment down in Florida. "Hey mom, how are you?" Desmarie asked her mother. "I am good, very good, are you ok?" Maria wondered and said aloud. Desmarie nods with confidence while taking a bite of her toast. She looks outside the window to the gleaming morning sunlight coming into the house. "I am going to the pool for a little bit, come with me mom!" Desmarie raises her voice with excitement as she gulps the last bit of orange juice from her mug. "Yes, I will be out there in a little bit and I will watch you, I still have to unpack our stuff," Maria remarks to her daughter as she steps into the living room.

Swimming in that pool felt so relaxing and fun. Although alone in that moment, Desmarie was having a much more fun time here compared to Florida. She felt relaxed and calm, but also stimulated to continue touring Victor's backyard which was 7 acres in size. Victor was a landscaper and had greenhouses in the backyard full of flowers. With the many good qualities that Victor had, one that tops everything was helping her quit the horrible habit of cigarette smoking. Maria of course fell in love with the yard and helped him grow, plant, and water daily. All the while maintaining contact with her kids in Florida.

CHAPTER 4

The First Summer in New Jersey

Desmarie's sister Babi and her brother came to visit the house in New Jersey months after the move. One late morning, Desmarie was helping her brother move a garden hose to the closest outside faucet in the wall to help water the potted plants out in the lawn. While walking in reverse and pulling the hose, Desmarie steps on it with one foot, trips and loses balance. She fell down onto the rocky terrain in the yard. She bears all of her body weight to her right upper side, placing the burden and poundage on her arm. Unfortunately, Desmarie got badly injured and began to cry out in pain. This was not a great start to living in a new and unfamiliar setting, as well as just being super uncomfortable in general. This was not a good way to begin her first summer in New Jersey either. "All I see are white stars, and I feel sharp and constant pain pulsating down my right arm!" Desmarie was crying out to her mom while trying to sit down inside. She cuddles her arm close and just closes her eyes, then opens, wincing in pain that wasn't coming to an end. "We have to see a doctor Victor, come on let's go!" Maria runs to the doorway to get her car keys, rapidly breathing with coughs covering the entire hallway. She turns on the engine to the car and pulls out of the garage, all while muttering "Shit!" towards the situation.

Walking out of the medical specialist's office, her right forearm is casted with a plaster-like material to help reposition the broken bone. A greenstick fracture to the right ulna. Desmarie was casted for 7 weeks, basically the entire summer. Overly angry and upset, she felt frustrated, discouraged, and all in all just mad. "I just can't believe it, I am so stupid!" mumbling under her breath to make sure it wasn't obvious but was still heard by her mother. Maria just looks down and caresses her daughter's head for reassurance.

They both get home, Desmarie goes to her room to rest. A couple of days pass, Maria comes into her room one morning and she leads Desmarie outside to walk a little bit and meet their next-door neighbors. Maria, holding Desmarie's hand, crosses the yard and steps onto their patio area next to their pool. "Hello! My name is Ruth and welcome to our home! Welcome to the neighborhood!" Their next-door neighbor gets close to them and speaks out, showing off a bright and cheerful expression to her face. Her rosy cheeks seemed gentle-like, but still, too much of a show right now at this moment when Desmarie was clearly in a bad mood. Not feeling up for it, she was simply just upset at herself about the whole thing; the whole accident. Maria pats Desmarie on her shoulder, and gives her a light nudge for her to move forward and introduce herself. "Manners Desmarie, say hi!" Maria grudgingly tells Desmarie in Spanish as she continues to put on a smile on her face for Ruth and everyone else there. The sound of splashing and small kids yelling in the background by the pool came at a disadvantage to Desmarie. These people seem nice, but I am just not in the mood right now. Desmarie's thoughts continue to cloud over her head, taking out the sight of what is actually happening in front of her right now. Ruth's daughter Lilly continues to play and giggles loudly with her other friends and cousins in the pool beside her. She catches sight of Desmarie and swims up to her. "Hey! I am Lilly, come in the pool with us!" Lilly's cute smile lights up their surroundings. The waves being made in the pool become larger as the kids' movement increases. Lilly was the social butterfly of the group, the little girl who always smiled and always spoke out about anything. This was truly a great way to start getting to know each other, but too bad Desmarie still felt embittered. "I am sorry you broke your arm, but here let me introduce you to my daughter Lilly and the rest of the gang," Ruth says, catching Desmarie off guard while walking alongside her mom to say hi to the family.

Desmarie's first summer in a new home was just like your average person's experience. Exciting, scary with some anxiety, overwhelming but in a good sense with new friendships being formed. The next-door neighbors were such good and genuine people. Individuals who carried such big hearts, and seemed to always put family first. Desmarie finally opened up to them and warmed up to Lilly. She would tell her the story of how she injured her arm, then play in the toy room, where Lilly had an endless number of toys to play with and share. This was so great, Desmarie thought. She would go over their house every day, which led to Lilly becoming her new best friend. They both would be inseparable when get-togethers took place during the holidays.

Maria would walk with Desmarie almost every night for her play date, then walk back home, returning later to get her daughter. Not much went on at home, Maria and Victor would spend their nights relaxing and watching television; usually game shows like Jeopardy, Wheel of Fortune, then maybe a click to change the channel over to a CSI investigation show. Desmarie, growing up as she was, was fully enjoying spending her time with Lilly and her family, but always loving to come back home and give her mom a big hug. Desmarie deep down was beginning to feel more and more grateful that she was able to move up north with her dear mother and make new friends; with people that were so kind about everything. From day 1, both Desmarie and Maria fell into the welcoming, warm, and embracing arms of their next-door neighbors. Their house was just as big, maybe a bit more than Desmarie's house. The kitchen always had food ready to eat, whether there were snacks or fresh cold-cuts out on a platter to serve up for sandwiches or small meals. At night time, entrees usually consisted of Desmarie's new favorite, pasta and chicken cutlets. If she was lucky enough to make it for lunch, she would be able to sit next to Lilly and eat Ruth's famous grilled cheese sandwiches. All in all, an amazing place to be in, a truly amazing time to spend with loved ones.

CHAPTER 5

A New Type of War

Everything was starting to fit like a puzzle and make sense in Desmarie's social life. Heck, she never really had a real social life, not often at least. After the summer ended, the cast finally came off, then school started. Desmarie began the 5th grade in New Jersey. Waiting at the bus stop at the end of the block would be quiet and warm in the spring/summers, cold in the fall/winter seasons; but always filled with the company of the rest of the neighbors from the block. Desmarie's sister Babi would be the only one visiting them in New Jersey more than once; usually small and big holidays throughout the year.

School was going great, Desmarie was beginning to feel more comfortable and felt welcomed in the new building. The students in all of her classes were also cool with her. Still shy and maintaining her timid personality, she made a few good friends, but stayed to herself mostly trying to maintain good grades to make her mother proud.

Tuesday morning, September 11 of the year 2001. It was unlike any other morning; it was strange. Desmarie continuously heard the principal in the loud speaker calling out to students to go down to the office. She figured that maybe they were in trouble, or were just caught up doing something they weren't supposed to be doing at the wrong place and time. But while passing the hallway, the principal kept beeping into the loud speaker, and the atmosphere began to change. It was getting quiet, there were no doors opening nor closing anywhere in the school building to go inside or out to the classrooms, none to exit the building.

Finally, the homeroom teacher gets up and tells the class to file up in a straight line and start walking to the cafeteria; no talking allowed. As Desmarie enters alongside her classmates, students are just whispering to each other, asking what is going on with the school. Waiting to get called down to the office herself, Desmarie clasps her hands together and just looks down. Yet no announcement was made to Desmarie on the overhead speaker. Desmarie ended up finishing the school day quickly as school buses began to park early outside to pick up students rapidly. It was an uneasy feeling all around because Desmarie still had no clue as to what was going on with this day.

Getting off the school bus, alone this time, Desmarie turns her key to unlock her front door. There she sees both her mother and step-father sitting on the couch in the den, watching the television very still. Their faces could be described as emotionless, shocked and frightened with cold sweat dripping down their faces. She could see her mom's hand trembling while the other hand was grabbing tight to Victor's who was sitting beside her. "A plane has crashed into one of the World Trade Center!" The reporter shouts out on live television with the intense chaos of yelling and screaming coming from the background. Maria grabs a hold of her daughter's hand to sit next to her and gives her a suffocating-like hug. Without letting go, Maria explains to Desmarie what had just happened. Maria and Victor were told to turn on their television from an incoming phone call from Spain; it was Desmarie's grandma! Her grandparents were seeing on TV the terrorist attacks happening in the U.S as it was happening, and made a frantic phone call to Desmarie's mother (their daughter) to let the family know.

The north tower collapses at the present time right now. Desmarie's face froze but had no words. She felt confused and nervous, she held on tight to her mother's hands. What is happening, why is this happening? Thoughts and questions circle around her mind, but all she could think about doing right now is just being with her mom, she hugged her tight. What happened on this day, 9/11, shocked all of the nation and changed the course of everything. "I can hear you; the rest of the world hears you. And the people who knocked these buildings down will hear from all of us soon." George W Bush said this as the president of the U.S. at the time. While all this was happening, Desmarie's head recoils and jerks forward from the effect of the strong coughing coming from Maria. The news seeming farther away as she watched her mother's chest continuing to bounce uncontrollably.

It was indeed a stressful and dark rest of the year, and it wasn't over. Maria's cough continued to worsen and her face began to look ill. Victor took her to the doctor to make sure she gets checked and receives the proper care and medicine to feel better. Unfortunately, this was not a simple cold nor even a small problem. This illness had gradually grown over the years, passed the 30 something years of cigarette smoking, pack after pack a day and it all led up to this. The word that absolutely no one wants to hear, the word that silently crawls up onto your shoulder, gives you a horrible tingling sensation and just doesn't leave you for a long time. Cancer.

CHAPTER 6

Underwater

Have you, being the reader of this book, ever experienced a feeling where you are running out of air to breathe? The feeling of being trapped, cold and toneless, stony-eyed like a statue? That was Desmarie. In that moment, from her eyes she saw darkness, a cloud of smoke surrounding her and grabbing onto mom; suffocating her. A force was pulling her away from mom. Desmarie started to close her mouth to be able to breathe through her nose again but all she smelled was rusted-like metal, then a whiff of rubbing alcohol, kind of like the last thing you smell before you lose consciousness and faint.

This was just a huge pill to swallow, as a matter of fact, impossible to swallow. What the fuck do we do now? What the fuck is going to happen? A fear that was always embedded in Desmarie's structure was fear of the unknown, death, and all of that stuff. Let's close our eyes and think about it for a minute or two. Desmarie was taken along by her mom and partner to go and live in a different place. She left her sisters and brother in Florida and went on to live with mom and Victor. Then, she meets these amazing people that lived next door to them. Day after day that passes, they become closer to each other, like family she never had growing up, but now to be a big part of the beginning of the adolescence stage. We are taking a mental road trip back in time because hey, this is what happens when horrible news gets broken down in front of you. You replay your life and rewind, to think about all the good that was happening and all of the good that was, until this. Everything was fine, Desmarie thought, but maybe it wasn't. Maybe nothing was fine at all, maybe this was just piling up. It became worse each day that passed, and Desmarie was too fucking blind to notice; everyone was too fucking blind to pay any attention. They didn't have their eyes open; the family was not being attentive as to what was happening daily right in front of them. The battle for life was slowly fading. Cancer might beat this battle that was happening inside a beautiful human being whose name is Maria, which 4 kids call mom. An innocent, heart-warming, kind and loving individual, who has done nothing wrong but care for her family and provide; provide to the extreme by which ever means necessary. She had finally met and married someone who was taking care of her, like no one, not even her ex-husband has ever done for her. And now this, this horrific change is happening, and Desmarie is NOT ready for this. She can't take care of herself, this is ridiculous, this shouldn't be happening, WHY is this happening? "I can't breathe," Desmarie's thoughts clouded over her conscious.

CHAPTER 7

Defeat

It's a confusing feeling. Guilt can rip you apart, it can cause anxiety and depression. A throbbing heart beat sound becomes overpowering inside Desmarie's head. It started to become louder and more disturbing.

Inside a hospital room, Maria was laying down on a hospital bed with an oxygen mask on. Victor by her side, reading a book. Desmarie was 11 years old now, she enjoyed reading as well. A couple of months pass by, Maria was admitted to the hospital around the beginning of the summer. This day today, Friday July 26, it was about 5:00pm in the evening and Desmarie was reading Black beauty- it was a book about a black horse. Desmarie couldn't concentrate much, as she turned the pages and just looked at pictures, she did not focus on the words, as the background noise kept interrupting. Maria was struggling to breathe even with an oxygen mask on, her legs kicking the tray of hospital food and jello to the floor in a brisk and rough manner. Victor calls the nurse to come and assist. Desmarie goes to her mom after the nurse gave her something to calm the anxiety, and holds her hand. Her hand felt sweaty, a little colder than room temperature, not usually her mom's hand. Desmarie begins to feel dread; realization that maybe her mom will not be ok, even though she remembers and is able to picture the doctor's face looking straight at Desmarie weeks ago, advising to her with these words exact, "Don't worry, your momma is going to be ok."

Why would he lie? He can't lie, he is a doctor. At least that's what an 11-year old's mind is going to think. But now, the ringing in her ears get louder, it's not clear. The real truth that was setting in felt like a big sack of bricks landing on top of Desmarie. As humans, we all tend to create a protective barrier so we don't get mentally hurt; so we can remain calm and ok. We all try to protect our emotions; shield ourselves from harm's way mentally. Desmarie sat back down, then looked at her mom. She felt confused and not really there; lost in the deep abyss underwater without any protective equipment on.

You know how it is described and said that the ill on their almost last day of living, they actually feel ok miraculously and somehow present to you like they were never sick to begin with? It has been heard and written that those moments are their last chance of normal communication, and God is letting you have one last time of normalcy with your loved one to essentially spend the last moment with them to say goodbye. Well, that was Saturday. Desmarie held her mom's hand, which was connected with multiple IV tubes, and just talked to her. They didn't speak about much but mostly just mentioning how much love they have for each other. Desmarie felt like an awkward state, pretty much like why are moments like this happening? But at the same time, these moments felt good and comfortable next to her mom.

The 5 stages of grief are: denial, anger, bargaining, depression, and acceptance. Desmarie stayed at the first stage for a while. Being only 11 years old, it hits hard, but at the same time, feels like no hit at all. It's like a shocked reaction in which you choose not to believe. Desmarie was right there. On Sunday, July 28th, 2002, both Desmarie and Victor have been in the hospital all morning. Maria was not doing well, she ended up being placed on a breathing machine, a life support to maintain stable vitals. Victor decided to take Desmarie to get something for lunch to help distract her, they went to Wendy's which was one of her favorite fast foods. While not having much of an appetite, they still ate but in silence. Victor's cell rings, he picks up but Desmarie's hearing is crowded with the sounds of traffic surrounding the restaurant and customers ordering food in line right behind them. Victor hangs up the phone and cleans up the table as he takes Desmarie's hand to go back to the hospital.

Both of them get back to the hospital, and receive some bad news in the waiting room. Maria had passed away. Desmarie stood there, silent, tongue-tied, her brain in limbo, her conscious in an oblivion of emptiness. She didn't know what to feel, all she heard was an echo of ICU machines beeping, rapid footsteps across the hallway of nurses attending to their patients. Her vision became blurry without any noise coming from the background. It was a moment of just…nothing. Defeat took control and won. "She's gone?" Desmarie quietly thought to herself. They both follow the doctor to her room where Maria was just lying there, mouth open, eyes closed, her skin gradually getting paler than before.

CHAPTER 8

Autopilot

Desmarie was shocked, she didn't believe it. All she was able to do to block out any incoming emotions was to keep asking questions to the doctor. "Is my mom not ok, what happened? Will she be going up to heaven, will she be ok? I don't understand?" No tears in sight, just questions after questions came up as if trying to comprehend something so dire. A lost child was standing in the ICU section of the hospital and made Desmarie feel as a cast away.

Coming home that day, Desmarie walks into the kitchen, then goes to her room and just sits on her bed and stares into space. Wondering what just happened, as a large amount of time passes. From recent memories, Desmarie did not have an appetite, did not think about food, drinking, sleep wasn't even in the agenda. The schedule was sitting on her bed, waiting. Waiting for a good explanation as to what is happening around her, waiting to hear back from her mom, waiting for hope. Waiting for Maria to come knocking on her door and saying hi. Yet she didn't come, none of it came. Nothing was good anymore, it's over. What is the point of living? "I'll just sit here," Desmarie thought.

Hours pass, outbound calls take place as Victor contacts each of Desmarie's siblings to tell them the bad news. Babi, who was just there in New Jersey for Easter in March, fainted to the ground when hearing the news. Everyone else presented with a shocking and horrified response. She was only 49 years old. No one should ever leave this earth that young. Not mom, not anyone! The morning after, Victor is in his bedroom and opens the closet door. He had to choose an outfit for Maria for her wake event. He grabs from a hanger and pulls out Maria's peach-colored wedding dress. "This was the dress she wore to our weddi..." his words come out in a mumble as he begins sobbing with tears cascading down his cheeks and moans aloud with sadness. Desmarie just stood at the doorway in silence, she never had seen Victor like this; completely broken. She didn't know what to say to him. She didn't know what to do now.

Desmarie got to see all of her siblings, as they had traveled to New Jersey to attend mom's funeral that following week. One of the nights, both Desmarie and her sister Babi walk over to Lilly's house. Ruth spends hours talking to both of them, speaking to them about the after-life, heaven, and signs. Signs of communication that Maria will be doing to Desmarie because that is what a mother-daughter relationship is having meant. Connection, love, protection, all of that is still present as Maria is still with us. Both Desmarie and Babi listen intensively. Ruth even brought up that Maria loved white butterflies, she loved being outdoors and just enjoyed looking at them flutter by throughout the day. Something that Desmarie didn't know, something that was taken for granted. She wasn't able to know this because she was doing something else. So many good things taken for granted. This positivity and reassurance that her spirit is with all of them made Desmarie feel hope and gave her faith. She slowly was getting picked up and escaping out of the dark hole that she has been trapped in for a week.

Sitting on top of a long and fancy leather seat, Desmarie felt uneasy. She had never ridden on a limousine before. And quite honestly, nobody wants their first limo ride to be the one where it takes them to a family member's funeral. The a/c was blasting in the back seats. Even without the cold air blowing onto her face, Desmarie felt cold. Her pale and clammy hands remained clasped together. Her right leg did not stop moving up and down rapidly. She looked outside her window to see the sun crashing to her eyes. Her eyes wincing, she sees clear again and notices all of the cars following them behind her. She then turns to look at the driver's seat and catches glimpse of 2 police officers guiding them into the cemetery. Desmarie feels her stomach hurt a little while taking a deep breath. The driver stops and unlocks the passenger doors from both sides, they had arrived.

The day had a clear blue sky, no winds whatsoever. Desmarie is sitting up front with her siblings, the immediate family. Behind them were close family and friends. Her next-door neighbors were sitting right behind them. Tears begin to seep down mostly everyone's' cheeks. Desmarie bites her bottom lip and gives in to her emotions, finally. Desmarie felt released, all of this built up anger and sadness were coming out in the form of tears. This was really happening, mom is right there, in front of her, being put inside a wall for memoriam. Desmarie will not be able to touch her anymore, she will not be able to hug and kiss her anymore, she will not be able to tell her that she loves her all while cuddling. Becoming a teenager is going to be hard for Desmarie without a mom, entering puberty for the first time without a mom is going to suck and be confusing, and just suck some more. Continuing life in general is going to be hard without her here with them.

After the service finished, people began to exchange a few words of condolences. Desmarie sort of walked away from the crowd and just wanted to be alone. A sight catches her attention, and Ruth sees Desmarie just standing by herself, looking at a small meadow with flowers and more graves following the path. Tears continue waterfalling down her face, and for a moment, she held her breath while gasping silently. She sees a white butterfly flutter by in front of her right side. "Oh my god, mom!" Desmarie keeps her thoughts to herself, but right away exhales in relief. "I am going to be ok," she looks down and grins, then turns around and comes back to the family.

While going home, Desmarie begins to remember the over-powering smell of flowers from the wake days ago. She didn't like the strong scent, from here on out she knew that she would have trouble smelling any kind of flowers from anywhere. Looking at her mom, laying down so still, her face seemed different. Obviously, it was the funeral workers or whoever that had to fix her up for the event, but it just didn't look natural. If anyone was to ever see a wake, attend the funeral of YOUR own family member, you would never believe it nor even know how to feel. It's rough, and all you feel are sharp stings all over your body. All Desmarie can remember is mom's face, struggling to breathe, how she looked lifeless next to all the machines in that hospital room, the fucking waiting room. Those pictures DO NOT go away, no matter how hard she tries to forget about it and attempts to dismiss them. It's all black and white, God why doesn't this go away? Desmarie tries to escape her past over and over again, but she just can't as it is and will always be embedded in her subconscious forever. It felt like such a long day, but thankfully, life goes on whether it's fair or not at the moment. Time that passes will help lighten the load, hopefully because it has to, right? Life is hard, and it was only going to get harder later. Isolation starts to begin carrying along with Desmarie due to the weight of sadness being with her as the days passed on, now and forever.

Continuing to go to church every Sunday with her step-father, Desmarie felt lonelier and sadder without mom being there. The hymns sung became depressing to hear, as it constantly reminded her of the death and loss of her mother. The experience was no longer the same, nor did it feel rewarding nor harmonious as it should feel. The announcements that were made daily after the sermon finished by the pastor, Desmarie no longer chose to listen to them. They would include requests from the people such as praying for a sick family member, or wishing best to someone going through a tough and challenging time in their life. It obviously doesn't work. There is no hope. Desmarie would think in her mind as she felt forced to attend weekly. She felt that there was no longer urgency to go. As far as an 11-year-old comes along, Desmarie could remain positive for herself but at the end will continue to feel hopeless; faith will continue to dwindle down. Even though it all felt lost, she remembers the conversation she had with Ruth, the white butterfly. It was seeing behind her eyes too. She also remembers a letter that her mom wrote while she was in the hospital. The letter that is kept in her silver keepsake chest in her room, read to her "I love you my precious daughter. I know you are strong and you will keep going." The letter was about a page long in length, but Desmarie continued to have that at the top of her mind. Those words were thought through and written by Maria to her youngest daughter to secure her comfort and keep her aware that it will be ok; she will be ok. When that letter was given to Desmarie by Maria a couple of weeks before she passed, it was after she had a laryngoscopy. Desmarie remembers Maria sounding hoarse and having tears fall down from her eyes while looking at her little girl. She wasn't sure if that was because her mom was crying from pain, or because she just finished having a long ass tube go through her nostril and into her throat. "How dare they make my mom feel like that and do these horrible things to her?" Desmarie groaned under her breath, upset. Desmarie's feelings of hatred towards the hospital grew as each day passed. Desmarie skimmed through the letter at the time but she didn't think anything of it; she really didn't know what was going to happen at the end, none of them did. Today, she chooses to keep her head up as she remembers the signs that come from up above: the white butterflies.

CHAPTER 9

Everything Happens for a Reason

Days and weeks pass, leaving behind the day of the funeral and everything that had happened before that horrible time. They say time gradually heals all wounds, now would you the reader, agree with that? Desmarie often thinks about this saying, and at times agrees, other times disagrees. You see, the problem with this, is that when you think about a dark time in your life, you re-live it, you get fucked again. Everything around you gets sucked up in this huge rainstorm of a twister and you end up having trouble getting out. Sometimes you get stuck in it and you can't get out. The memory feels more powerful than the day of the horrific event that took place...why? Do our minds exaggerate emotions? Of course. Our subconscious stores emotionalized thoughts, hopes, and desires. It's sometimes good but sometimes bad. Desmarie knows now that her new stasis is older and wiser. There has to be moments like this, in order to make you stronger, come out more vigorous than how you started it. All in all, it was just a shitty situation. Desmarie tried to think about all of the conversations she had with her mom, and the ones they never got to have or will have again. All of the time now, she wishes for more time. Desmarie only had 11 years with her mom, so little time, but the impact Maria made in her life was astronomical. "There is a strength in you that you haven't even begun to find. And that's often how life works. You won't know how strong you are until the world forces you to look" (Blake Auden, 2020).

A teenager now, Desmarie is finishing up middle school and about to start high school in the upcoming month. Both Lilly and Desmarie ended up seeing each other daily. They have hung out and went to the movies, mall, shopping, got their nails done, watched MTV together, and all of the above. Lilly had become Desmarie's best friend. Being with Lilly gave Desmarie a sense of comfortability that wasn't there anymore ever since mom died. They both have become sisters. It was thanks to her next-door neighbors that Desmarie stayed alive.

Not so long ago, she was trapped inside a dark place, and did not show any signs of coming out; she was lost and didn't bother escaping the darkness. In the brink of becoming almost nothing and nonexistent, dead to be precise, Ruth and Nick who is her husband (Lilly's father) and Duke who was Lilly's older brother came to the rescue. Ruth took over being a mom and ended up teaching Desmarie so many life lessons and cared for her. She taught her each day how to live life to the fullest, allow room to make mistakes so she can learn from them, and primarily provided her all the good qualities of a real close family; what a true family should be. In this stage of life, Desmarie has come to realize that blood isn't everything. Desmarie always thought it was funny and weird, how she ended up in a neighborhood block, in the middle of nowhere in central Jersey, living next-door to these people that ended up being undercover guardian angels. Desmarie's story wasn't ending, it was just beginning. Maria would have wanted her youngest, to be happy. What is hope in this world we live in? What is hope in the world that Desmarie lives in? Well, we can start with having people we love around us. We can look ahead; everything eventually starts coming together like a puzzle. Everything also starts to make sense. Desmarie gradually learned and continued to learn putting off things that made her sad, and tried to be optimistic when she was able to be as she got older. When you lose something close to you, the thing that pulls you off from that darkness is love. And that, ladies and gentlemen, were her next-door neighbors.

CHAPTER 10

Growing Up

Being a teenager and living with her step-father, who was an older man, was difficult. Try imagining yourself being a teenage girl, living with a male senior citizen; it's not an easy thing to do. She had to be cautious as to where you hang the bath towel, in other words, make sure it's hanging on left rack like he wants it and not on the right. Being nitpicky with so many little things, realistically it didn't make Desmarie's life easier. If anything, it made her feel more frustrated as the days went on. She didn't feel comfortable being at her own home.

Victor and Desmarie had a complicated relationship, there were many disagreements in which ended up pushing Desmarie away from him. It was an imperfect bond for someone taking care of another. All of the trauma built throughout recent years, made living in that house intense and just an all-around emotional rollercoaster ride. Just walking into mom's bedroom was painful, it gave Desmarie a queasy feeling in her stomach that would last the remainder of the day. It wasn't pleasant nor easy to deal with. Desmarie's only escape was going next door. Her daily elopement was being with her second family, the people that were able to relate a bit more due to being closer in age; especially Lilly being 4 years younger who was like a little sister to Desmarie. They both spent so much time having hundreds of conversations that were just so necessary to have in that age group for girls. Those simple moments in time were needed for Desmarie, those hang outs were essential to have in her life, and let's put into perspective; for Lilly as well.

Now with many fun memories, having regrets also came to place. Desmarie spent a lot of time in her head thinking what could have been. The fault in us humans, is that we take things for granted. We leave each other, the ones we care for, in the dark for so long that they end up becoming part of it. All Desmarie wanted to have was peace and comfort, not people who keep her in a constant state of unrest and doubt. All of us think about being happy ourselves and that's it, we're all selfish in so many ways. Of course, being a teenager with raging hormones being felt constantly didn't make it any easier. Having her neighbors though as guidance, in addition to Victor also keeping a roof over her head with meals prepared was good enough for her; she is still alive.

Desmarie had the pleasure to be able to visit her close sister Babi in St. Thomas who lived in the US Virgin Islands; America's paradise. From the end of middle school, moving quickly onto high school, Desmarie was able to visit her for almost all of her spring break weeks in the years coming, and of course about 6-8 weeks for the summers. Definitely not complaining about her current situation, Desmarie was glad she was able to do these things. She was able to keep close contact with the closest sister from Florida who in many ways was just like their mom; at least she reminded Desmarie a lot of their mom. The closeness they shared had always helped them and made them feel good in each other's presence.

Both Lilly and Desmarie got closer to each other throughout high school. Desmarie learned that Ruth was the kind of mom that every girl could ever want in life. Super down to earth and lenient, but also remained strict when she had to be to keep her family safe. Ruth provided her kids with a life style of letting her kids have fun, but also letting them learn from their mistakes; it becomes a lesson learned type of thing. Desmarie grew up being perfectly fine with it. Curfews would still be in effect for their house, but it was a lot more forgiving compared to Victor's household rules.

In the winters when it snowed, Lilly and Desmarie would go snow-sledding down Victor's big hill in his yard. Desmarie would attempt to snow board but would always fall flat on her face. Coming inside the house would be so funny, as Desmarie would step onto pages from a newspaper all over the floor and going up and down steps. It was mainly to retrieve the snow from coming further into the house where the carpet was from the shoes. Taking off her snow boots, she and Lilly would walk into the kitchen where Ruth would already have hot chocolates ready for them. They would be served at times through the window when the girls would still be hanging outside like a drive thru. Duke would sometimes run outside and start a snowball fight with both girls but Desmarie ended up always being his target to getting her face smashed into the snow. She did hate that, but in all honestly, it didn't bother her much because she had fun. She wouldn't trade this sibling play for anything else; it was a bond that Desmarie never really experienced with her own siblings in Florida. She wished she would have had a brother like Duke. Intense when it came to competitiveness but someone to teach Desmarie how to be tough in hard situations, besides being both serious and playful. He even showed the little big things like chivalry and protection to Desmarie. She really felt like she was part of this family; she was given a second family. But this time, it was a family to be with her in the good and bad; not just because they had to but because they wanted to.

A family is the most important aspect of life. Sometimes having a big family is helpful when it comes to dodging loneliness. But who determines if they will be there for you when you need them the most? Not you nor the size of the family. Just because you have 3 kids, 4 kids or more, doesn't necessarily mean you being one of the siblings will be super close with them always. Many people in this world confuse situations and events like that. Sometimes you just need one good sibling next to you, or even 2 close ones that will be and remain trustworthy to you. This family provided both emotional and economic support for Desmarie.

CHAPTER 11

Baby Girl

Nick is Lilly's father that was also growing to be and becoming Desmarie's second father. Before this story gets into the relationship of Nick and Desmarie while symbolizing father and daughter rapport, let's pause for a moment and think back. Desmarie's next-door neighbors took Desmarie in like their own. People around the world frequently see this a lot in movies and also read about them in fairy tale stories. But in reality, the way this family reached out to Desmarie and offered her help was beautiful. The tendencies that this world has during these last couple of decades are nothing like this story. It has become super hard to find a loving family like this who would without hesitation, invite a young kid into their home and be willing to invest and secure anything and everything needed for him/her. These wonderful beings didn't do it out of pity, it was with the kindness of their hearts that incepted Desmarie. There were times where Desmarie herself acted distant when it came to physical contact with the family, especially from both Ruth and Nick. Hugs and kisses were hard to accept from Lilly's parents, but why was that? Desmarie presenting an aloof personality like that just didn't make sense, or did it? What happens when a person loves someone an outstanding amount? I might get hurt again; they might just leave me without me being prepared for it. I might get my heart broken again. Loss, this is what happens when you care. Desmarie's thoughts continued clouding her judgement and was taking away the clarity; which is that this family loves her. Her cognition wasn't as clear in the moment, pessimism was emerging more and more into her imagination; it was deafening. She lost her mom and her heart broke into a million pieces; this has had no fix. She got hurt, and until this very day today, Desmarie is still very heavily bruised. This is what happens when you care and love; you get hurt. "What if I lose them too? I can't do this. Ugh! I don't know what I am doing, what's happening to me?" Desmarie begins to hold her stomach and show grimace. During those moments, she would walk back home to space herself out from them for a little while. Desmarie built a barrier in front of herself; metaphorically of course. She thought she would be protected this way. She was comfortable now, somewhat ok. Although she craved a mother's touch, a family's touch, she denied it in her mind and stopped herself from wanting it, or at least she tried.

During school nights when Desmarie would be over and in Lilly's room, Ruth would knock at the door and come inside with two bowls of spaghetti made with their homemade marinara. Handing Desmarie's bowl to her, she would sometimes reach over and give her a kiss on her head. Desmarie in the moment would mentally create a shield. The moment where Nick strokes her long dirty blonde hair and smiles while showing that father-like lovely smirk and says, "I love you baby girl." Her heart stops for a brief moment. It's hard to believe that this is what is healing her. Love. She is going to fall for it and accept it, but fall for what? Family? Love and acceptance? Desmarie remembers one day where Ruth was talking to her, and while giggling, she stumbles the words, "I know honey that if there were 10 older women standing in a horizontal line with me in it, and you had an opportunity to choose a mother based on appearance, you sure as hell wouldn't pick me," Ruth laughs hysterically but Desmarie stays looking serious. "Oh my goodness don't say that, that makes me feel horrible," Desmarie murmurs. Stating the obvious, but silently thinking, shit that might be true. "No Ruth, that's bullshit. I would be a complete idiot to miss the chance to have you as my mom, you are like my guardian angel, and Maria loved you so much." Looking at Ruth standing right in front of her, Desmarie goes up to her and plants a huge hug on her. "Thank you,

Ruth, I wouldn't change anything about you, everything about you is so great and I love you so much," Desmarie begins to get watery eyes as Ruth squeezes her tightly. Desmarie has her ear against her chest and hears her heartbeat. What a beautiful human being, and amazing mom she is, Desmarie closes her eyes in a daydream.

For her entire life growing up, Desmarie had no father nor did she even know the feeling of being a daddy's little girl. Her father from blood was in Spain with someone else, left her mom with 4 kids to go work on a "project" in Colombia. He never came back for her; he never came back for his family. To put it in simple terms, he was a piece of shit. Listed on her birth certificate, her father appears, but that's about it; nothing else to care about. As Desmarie grew up, he wasn't deserving to be in her life anymore. He wasn't even there to visit Maria when she was sick in the hospital. There weren't any phone calls nor any forms of communication to his family in New Jersey; absolutely nothing. He didn't even go to Maria's funeral. Fuck him.

With God's help and guidance, Desmarie ended up living in the same block as another neighborly family who ended up becoming her best friends, her saviors. This enormous support team that wasn't going to leave her stranded anytime soon. Desmarie can finally depend on them; she was able to see that. After some time passed, she finally accepted the hugs, the kisses, and all of the above. Things were getting normal and Desmarie was becoming her own person for the first time ever.

CHAPTER 12

Summer Nights

The girls would go to sleep late because it would stay light out till late; summers were so much fun. Swarms of pretty fireflies surrounded their back yard throughout the warm weeks. Lilly and Desmarie spent summer days and nights together daily. Going to Six Flags parks, usually Great Adventure which was the theme park to go to, would be a casual outing for them. Desmarie out of the two would feel more of a coward at times, especially the fact that Lilly was the one who would pull her to ride the crazy rollercoasters. One of them being Medusa which was an upside-down rollercoaster that was newly built in the park. Peer pressured to go to a scary ass ride, but it ended up being the best type of peer pressure, getting it from a younger sister and best friend. Desmarie finally grew guts and moved her legs along while running with Lilly to ride it. Twelve years old and finally, has ridden an upside-down rollercoaster. Meanwhile, Lilly was 8! Embarrassing but insane at the same time. It was actually starting to get easier becoming happy all over again. Hanging out with Lilly took all of the stress away. Lilly helped Desmarie conquer all her fears. It felt good being with her.

One summer night, Lilly was dribbling a basketball in her yard and was about to shoot the ball into the basket, but instead decided to do a random dance move while carrying the ball and she pivoted her hips awkwardly. Her right ankle twisted when her body veered to the right and she bared all of her weight there. Falling down to the ground, Lilly screams, "Ouuuuuchh!" Feeling severe pain, Lilly's rosy and freckled cheeks get covered up with tears. "Shit, Lilly are you ok?" Desmarie runs up to Lilly where Ruth was already standing over her and helping her up. "We need to go to the ER right now, her ankle is swollen and purple but we need to get something to help her get around in the meantime," Ruth helped Lilly up and began to rub her foot while moving the ankle slowly. Shit, shit! What do we do now? Desmarie was scrambling, she kept looking around to see if there was anything they can use. She suddenly then glances from afar at her garage(s) in her yard at Victor's. The pitch black did not welcome any bit of light, as it became bigger and more fearsome, but Desmarie ignored her apprehension and started running towards her yard. Desmarie swears she heard whispers in the dark but they were just insects outside. As the scary noises became louder, probably in her head, she sped up and ended up running into her garage entrance passed the door. "Fuck, fuck, where are you? Crutches, wheelchair, give me something, anything!" Desmarie growls in frustration as she kept stumbling over random tools thrown on the ground. Starting to slightly give up, she heads towards the exit but then looks up in front of her and sees Lilly from a distance. She sees Lilly on the ground again holding her ankle while rocking back and forth, squirming with the agonizing burning sensation in her swollen ankle. Desmarie hears her screams and notices them fading as the bugs outside become louder in the night. She grunts and gets angry then turned back around and resumed looking. She yelled at Ruth to please keep talking to her and to make noise so she would feel less scared while looking through the dark cluster of things filling up the garage. Finally, after several minutes in there, Desmarie felt with her hands some old crutches leaning against the corner wall of one of the entrances. While shaking them and getting the spider webs off, she yelled, "Oh thank god. Guys I am coming! I found crutches!" Desmarie yelped out to both Ruth and Lilly. She ran back to them and helped Lilly up with the crutches at hand. They ended up finally going to the ER, where they diagnosed Lilly with an acute sprained ankle. "Wow Desmarie, that was really brave of you," Ruth pats Desmarie on her shoulder. Not even really listening to what Ruth was saying, Desmarie kept holding onto

Lilly's hand and making sure she was ok. On the drive home, Lilly was falling asleep. Desmarie was sitting in the back seat next to her. She kissed her forehead and rests her chin on Lilly's head. "I'll always be by your side. I'll fly with you" (Gigi D' Agostino, 1999). Desmarie closes her eyes as she falls asleep too.

Lilly and Desmarie always had sleepovers together. It was a must during short and long weekends off from school. Falling asleep together in the same bed while talking, Lilly would leave her room messy just because it didn't matter when Desmarie was there. Letting yourself go and just having fun is the way to live, but many times Ruth didn't like the mess. Summer nights toasting marshmallows in the backyard, putting the burnt marshmallow on a graham cracker with Hershey's chocolates in between; eating yummy smores. Movie theater nights at the mall, spending only $6-8 for a movie ticket and like $4 for a large popcorn. Eating nachos and Raisinets and M&Ms in the freezing cold theater, but having the popcorn warm you up was awesome. Getting drunk on the good life, either at home hiding in Lilly's bedroom while they sneaked bottles inside without Ruth nor Nick finding out, or just drinking outside in the hot tub and pool. Desmarie grew her trust with Lilly, even letting her pierce her second holes in both ears while being piss drunk in the toy room. Using a lemon just like they showed it in the classic movie The Parent Trap, although Desmarie was still confused (and drunk) as to why the lemon was useful in that scenario. Participating in school variety shows were also so much fun to do together. Ruth would take the girls to rehearsals and be at home trying out outfits to mix and match, while practicing dance routines for the show coming up.

Summer nights consisted of both sisters lying on the couch in the living room watching shows on TV, or in Lilly's room blasting the Disney Channel if they were in a playful mood, even watching MTV music videos if they felt like rebels. Desmarie would always be thinking of good memories from previous summers. She remembers when Ruth had told her that a white butterfly was flying around Lilly and closing in on her while she was just standing by her pool. Lilly called out to her mom in a shocked tone of voice, as the white butterfly got closer to her. Then, all of a sudden, it lands on her nose. Maria. That was Desmarie's mom. A clear sign that she was with all of them always. Maria always had a gentle love and connection with Lilly, as if she was her other young daughter.

Summer nights would be swimming in Lilly's pool, sometimes even Desmarie's pool if Ruth wasn't home and they had no other choice. Both girls would have fun skinny-dipping in Lilly's pool during the night and mess around while playing pool games; laughing at random shit that comes to mind. The underwater amusement they had was great.

CHAPTER 13

High School

Ah, the good old days, right? Hah, it wasn't always good. The culture in high school could be described as confusing, fun, exciting, stressful, awful but enjoyable in too many instances. High school is not nearly as bad as movies depict it to be on screen. When you think about cliques, it really is just certain people that always hang out with each other. Desmarie kept a close circle with close friends, but friends didn't always get along with other friends; that was the problem. Peer pressure follows along after that, of course. With everyone having a unique and different personality, sometimes two people just didn't go well together, whether it was for a relationship of dating, or just simply a friendship. Desmarie would always try to play equal, sometimes sit next to the varsity team in lunch, sometimes stay with the nerdy fun friends, but always be there for her people in general. That was important in high school. Bullying also took place, unfortunately in everyone's lives. There is always at least one instance in every student's school life that has an encounter with a bully. You can be doing everything right and the way you are supposed to, but it still happens, simply because not everyone will like you. That is life. Nobody is perfect. There was even a point where Desmarie thought she liked girls because she thought one of her friends was really pretty. But when it came down to it during a party at another friend's house, she couldn't move forward after the one kiss because she simply wasn't interested in that way anymore, it was just pure curiosity at the moment as it struck. Luckily, the friendship with her still lasted even after high school; that phase pretty much ended. Along with that, many confusing moments took place during high school, but Desmarie made sure to stay strong and tackle any obstacle that came her way. One that wasn't so easy to dodge was peer pressure, and believe her, there was no way of escaping peer pressure. It would follow her in school and even outside during shopping and dates.

Desmarie sometimes had to escape from all of the craziness, come home, toss her Jan Sport backpack on the floor and walk over next door. Lilly wouldn't be home yet, but sometimes she would just be in her room playing with her phone or watching TV, waiting for her best friend to get home. Desmarie enjoyed those days, freshmen-sophomore year where she didn't have a driver's license yet but was soon going to take Driver's Ed class. She got to spend a lot of time with Ruth as well, just talking about random stuff. These moments were priceless and were dearly missed since her mom left when Desmarie was 11. If there was an imaginary button that would pause these moments, Desmarie would have pushed it a while ago. Being with good friends also had a big impact in her life. It became worthwhile during school days and beyond that. Being around people close to age that one can connect with, communicate and share things with is amazing; all while sleeping over friends' houses to exchange gossip all night.

Desmarie's family next-door helped her break out of her shell and enter the real world, where not everything was sunshine and rainbows all of the time. They made her become a more social person, and face the universe while lessening her fears little by little. God, if that isn't family, if that isn't love, then what is? What do you live for? This beautiful family made Desmarie become a better person. During these times in life, it was crucial for Desmarie to experience it all and be a part of something worth living. Sometimes, we all have to come out and discover things for our own. We all have to learn some way and unfortunately, sometimes it's the hard way. But one thing is for certain, Desmarie regrets nothing. As one gains many friendships, some others get lost in the shuffle. Desmarie made sure to stay imminent to her best friends; the ones that were always there for her. She once had a good friend who had the same name as her mom, and was just a really down-to-earth girl. Desmarie one time got out of gym class and while going to her next class, she noticed that Maria's ring that would always be worn was not on her finger. Desmarie cried for most of that day. Walking to last period class in the hallway, her friend spotted her and immediately noticed her red and swollen eyes. She came over to give Desmarie a big hug and reassured her that she will be ok, and it might just appear out of nowhere. Crazy to mention, that same night which was a Friday night, Desmarie slept over her best friend's house Marie. They both were Friends fanatics (the TV show) and would always watch that together, along with playing SIMS in the computer and just hanging out. When changing to her PJs, Desmarie noticed something small and hard inside her sneaker while taking them off. Mom's ring! Whoa, an unbelievable miracle happened. The feeling of relief swept Desmarie off the ground. She stepped out of the bathroom and screamed with joy.

Desmarie gets out of the school bus and drops her stuff off at home, then goes next-door. Lilly was home, she wasn't feeling too good. She suffers sometimes with her asthma, so Ruth makes sure that she is taken care of throughout the day. Desmarie goes into her room and shuts the door. Being with Lilly, now we are talking about a really special person here. Lilly from being super young once, now has become a teenager herself. She ended up blossoming into a great girl and best friend to have; a sister. Desmarie was able to be her complete self with her and they both told each other everything. It ended up being a rare type of bond that these girls developed. Unlike being with a friend for some time, it didn't get tiring nor old. It evolved into a special connection like sisters that didn't know were sisters. Where one of them would jump in front of a bullet for the other. Desmarie always thought and ended up taking to account that these people saved her life.

From parties and get togethers, to being with the rest of the family, Desmarie was happy. She was comfortable and she was living life. Lilly never had to lie to Desmarie. Some days even called when it came time to have a brutally honest conversation with each other. It would pass and the result was either someone getting mad at the other and leaving the house, but then coming back a day later to visit. Or they get upset then get over it and continue talking.

"You know, I think we have been sisters in another world. But in this universe, I think we discovered our sisterly bond later than sooner, and I fucking love you Lilly!" Desmarie told Lilly excitedly as they take shots of rum in the hot tub. "Haha Desmarie, stop saying that I saved you, come on, you are so strong and I just really look up to you. I would have never been able to deal with all the shit you coped with through these years," Lilly looks down and takes Desmarie's bottle of rum to take another drink. These were the one and a million of sleepovers that were unforgettable. Evenings like this are meant to forget about the stress and just live and laugh.

For the readers out there, this would like to be expressed: Blood is not thicker than water. Meaning, don't think nor assume that blood family will be there through thick and thin all the time. In a lifetime, one will come across to meet a large number of people. Some of them will stick around for a little while and then leave, others will just like a gust of wind that comes and disappears like a quick breeze; so fast to go in and out of your life that you will barely remember them in the future. But then, if you're lucky enough like Desmarie, you will get to meet some wonderful people who end up becoming your family. They will be there through it all with you, holding your hand and helping you survive.

During junior year in high school, Desmarie got into a car accident. It was her very first crash while driving a car that was provided to her by Ruth. Yes, she was spoiled but as a high schooler, teenagers don't realize how good they really have it. They don't focus much on appreciation in the long-term, just expressing gratitude for the moment, if anything. The car accident happened in such a plain and foolish manner; but what auto accident nowadays doesn't? Desmarie and one of her best friends from school decided to start racing each other once they entered the friend's neighborhood one afternoon after school. While driving and zooming past houses, going at an obvious high speed at about 45 mph (35mph being the limit), Desmarie ran a stop sign. About 2 feet passing the street sign, Desmarie remembers seeing a flash of green across the street; in front of her eyesight. Staying steady at a fast speed, Desmarie suddenly crashes against the green jeep Cherokee, hitting the right rear hard. The air bags in the front miraculously deployed in Desmarie's old sonata. Her eyes were stayed shut for a little while, then they slowly opened to see a rainbow mix of white and grey smoke in front of her. The ringing in her ears did not want to stop, it was coming from both sides. As Desmarie motions to open her eyes wider, she sees her best friend get out of her jeep and run up to where she was. "Oh my god, oh my god, Desmarie are you ok?!" her friend is gasping for air as she nervously forces open Desmarie's door to check on her. With some struggle, the door finally opens. Desmarie mumbles and nods slowly to confirm that she was ok. No scratch was seen on Desmarie in that moment. She actually wasn't sure if she was hallucinating but she remembers seeing a white butterfly from a distance fly by in the scene of the accident, then disappearing. Her friend's jeep was dented pretty bad, but nothing serious that a repair shop wouldn't be able to fix. After all, it was a giant SUV compared to Desmarie's small sedan. The sonata ended up being completely totaled. Examining the front, it was conclusive to say that it was destroyed with the bumper hanging. Fuck! This just happened. Cops were called from both sides. In the moment sometime after, Desmarie also reached out to her neighbors to share the bad news. Being perceptible and all, Ruth and Nick were upset but glad that Desmarie was ok; hard to believe she only ended up with some pain in the neck from the whip lash motion in the impact. The ringing begins to faint finally and while going away, Desmarie continued looking around and listening to the female police officer that just got there. This was a near-death experience for Desmarie. If she would have driven a bit faster, and her friend a bit slower, she would have hit Desmarie directly on the driver's side; striking her entire body. Also knowing at that time, it was doubtful that the old Hyundai sonata even had side airbags since they never popped out after the crash. Desmarie got a ticket from the officer since she did run a stop sign. Angry at the current situation, Desmarie knew that she was on her own with fixing this debacle. She really messed up, and there was no way that she would be given another car. After this event happened, Desmarie little by little began to figure out what the value of a dollar was and meant. She would have to look for a job to start earning money to get herself another car. Let's all be serious here, a high-schooler needs to be driving their car during senior year. If not, that would just be embarrassing for everyone.

CHAPTER 14

A Close Call

The summer before senior year began, was one of the most nerve-racking and stressful times that took place. Desmarie received a call from Ruth while she was still visiting her sister Babi in St. Thomas, USVI during that summer; the summer before senior year. Helping her sister at work at the time, she answered the call and almost dropped the cellphone. "Hey sweetheart, I don't know where to start but honey I saw all of your stuff thrown into Victor's garage. I am not exactly sure why it has happened but his granddaughter came and wanted to claim your room for herself. She felt like you shouldn't be living there and "mooching" off of him since you aren't his real family." Ruth continues to anxiously blurt what was happening out to Desmarie in such a worrisome tone of voice. Listening from the other end of the telephone was not easy. "Wait, wait, I don't understand, what the fuck is going on?" Desmarie begins to shake with her nerves twitching with anger all over. Desmarie stays quiet. She begins to think about Victor's family. He had 5 kids with regards to one passing away years ago. The 2 daughters and one son disliked Maria and her kids; the entire family to shorten it. All but one son ended up actually caring for Desmarie. The rest she guessed felt some kind of jealousy? Like Maria sort of stole Victor from them; but not really? Given the details from the past, Victor's first spouse was with him for a long time but passed away from an illness caused by smoking. Two years later, he meets and then ends up falling head over heels in love with Desmarie's mom Maria. These events were things that Desmarie couldn't control, I mean, nobody can control. At the end of the day, Desmarie was just a child and she was innocent. She would not have chosen to transpire pain and suffering for anyone, not even her enemies. You also can't control who you fall in love with for god sake! Desmarie was now 17 years old and about to finish high school and graduate from a long and mentally exhausting road she has been in all this time. She has also had the blessing of meeting her next-door neighbors who became her family. Everything was fine and like it was mentioned earlier, she has now one more year of school left before deciding what she wants to do with the rest of her life.

Desmarie in the moment stood shocked and confused. She knew that part of his family did not like her, but come on! Who in their right mind does this to someone; a minor?! "Please Ruth, talk to Victor, please, I don't even know what to say right now, what happens now? Do I stay here? Do I go back to Miami? And with school? What the fuck am I supposed to do?" Desmarie tries to calm herself and prevent herself from having a panic attack. Babi begins to worry but starts to think and reason as to why this was happening. Babi is a kind soul who always looks for the good in people, but sorry to say, there was no good in this individual that was literally throwing Desmarie's belongings outside to the fucking garage. If Desmarie was to come back now to New Jersey, she wouldn't even have her bed to sleep in, as that piece of furniture was also tossed to the garage. "What the fuck is wrong with her? What did I ever do to her? Why isn't Victor doing anything about this? Is he just sitting there and letting her do what she wants? "Of course, it's his family; his true family I guess," Desmarie told herself. She is Victor's step-daughter, and just like the story of Cinderella, step children don't mean shit apparently. Just throw me out of your life I guess, Desmarie continues to think and wonder. Towards the end, she honestly just doesn't know what to do to fix this. All she did that entire day was beg Ruth over the phone to please try and do something to help because this just can't be happening; not now. For crying aloud, Desmarie is not even there in person to see what is going on.

Ruth went over to see Victor. She tried to talk and reason with him about these actions. Victor for unknown reasons just didn't give. She was confused as to why all of a sudden this was happening; as all of this was just baffling. After several attempts to change his mind, the result was going to just let this happen since there was no other choice apparently. Desmarie is going to have to move to Miami with maybe one of her siblings, that to be honest had their own lives and Desmarie would be feeling unwanted and just be intruding in their lives.

With dark clouds setting in, there was a ray of sunshine still peeking through the stormy nebulosity outside. Duke, who is Lilly's older brother, went to talk with Victor some days after to supervene. He essentially told Victor that this couldn't happen, that it would ruin Desmarie's future, life, and all that she worked for here. She would lose her credits from school, would have to start all over and have to say good-bye to all of her friends. This was cruel, and there had to be some other way to change course and leave this madness behind that was happening. Ruth found out what Duke had done and shared the news to Desmarie, but not expecting any change to happen. Ruth also tried to talk to him once more again about stopping this and to find a more peaceful way to go about this; hopefully a better solution. But not even a nudge.

Miracles do happen and eventually after weeks passed, before school started and before the summer break ended, Victor finally accepted into a mutual solution. A quick fix that would not require any effort whatsoever for their neighbors to do. Take Desmarie in to live with them. Have Desmarie do something that she basically is already doing, which is to live in their house permanently and be supported by them. Adoption or obtain guardianship, those were the choices being filled in Ruth's mind. How unbelievable, what rarity! Ruth contacts Desmarie to let her know. Desmarie drops to a chair and lets out a big sigh of relief. Her leg continues bouncing up and down rapidly as she tries to juggle all of the events that happened in two weeks. "Thank you, mom," Desmarie prays with her eyes closed. Her hands stay clasped together and she begins to cry with emotions that are overpowering and overwhelmingly large to contain any longer.

Desmarie remembers catching the plane to go back home to New Jersey, looking out the window from her window seat and staring at the cloudy and limitless sky surrounding the plane. Desmarie closes her eyes and dozes off into a pleasant sleep. The sun setting in the sky had orange and yellow splashes of color, being filled with the darkness arising in the distant horizon. "My God, you are beautiful," admiring the sunset skies, Desmarie gets her phone out and ready to dial Ruth. The plane begins to prepare for landing. A phenomenon of hope arose that week, and she knew it was her mom alongside God's doing. Desmarie paints Victor's facial expression on her head, imagining how he would be looking at her right now. Thinking to herself, "I owe myself the biggest apology for putting up with shit I don't deserve," she lets out a sigh. Desmarie quickly changes her thought in mind and moves on. Actions speak louder than words. To all audiences, next time someone tries to convince you that they care, look at what they do, not what they say.

Coming home, Desmarie remembers hugging Ruth and Nick so tight when she saw them. If someone was pointing to them with a camera, they can tell you this. The event shown through the lens, portrayed a desperate teenager crying and longing for her parents after not seeing them for years. That's what it felt like. You don't know what you got until it's gone. Desmarie was so close to losing her family in New Jersey. Saying farewell to everything familiar to her; saying goodbye to the life she loved. This family, her neighbors, were not only there for her in the past, but now, they are literally saving her life AGAIN. All of them are a blessing from the heavens. Desmarie continues to wonder the possibility that could have happened in tears, while in relief as she tightly holds onto Ruth in a big warm embrace. A huge boulder was pulled off from the top of her, it was suffocating Desmarie at one time with fear covering her up. What a close call, in one moment everything is fine, the next moment was going to be all turned to shit. Desmarie almost lost it all again and she still doesn't even recognize the reasoning to this. Desmarie eventually stopped stressing at this situation and just started thinking positive from here on out.

The morning came when Ruth had to go to court and was asked to confirm with Victor for guardianship of Desmarie. She had to finish her schooling, there really was no good reason to just throw everything away now; and for absolutely no reason! Why not make a less risky solution? One that will not make anyone suffer deeply and full of regret. Why not make everyone comfortable and happy? Isn't that what matters, what should matter at least? The fault in us is that we the people hold hatred and grudge to some individuals, when acting foolish and dumb enough that most of the time is for reasons uncontrolled. Jealousy and hatred, they are both negative. To be quite honest, all of that shit just shortens a person's lifespan; or at least that's what it feels like. It isn't healthy, it's just plain sinful. Everyone is born good and innocent, until something bad happens.

Ruth finally comes home from the courthouse. Both Lilly and Desmarie were in the bedroom watching TV and eating a bowl of cereal. Lilly kept switching the channel until she got to MTV and saw her favorite music artist Panic! At The Disco, singing "I Write Sins Not Tragedies". Ruth grabs the remote control to lower the volume, then tries to get the girls' attention. In her hands, she holds up some paperwork from the court; confirming guardianship success. Desmarie jumped out of the bed with joy and gave her a big kiss. She was so grateful to be able to officially live with them and stay in New Jersey for the last year of school. What would happen afterwards, honestly, Desmarie didn't know. With the goodness of her family's heart, they provided Desmarie with a shelter as long as needed. That, my friends, is family. And one of the many things Desmarie was grateful for was not ending up in an orphanage; that would have changed her completely. To be clear, it would not have been for the better.

The toy room that was located in the back of the house, was organized and cleaned up to become Desmarie's new bedroom. Nick and Ruth set up a bed with a desktop computer connected for school work, as well as for talking with friends on AOL and AIM. Nick also mounted a 24" TV in the corner of the wall. Desmarie felt so happy and so at home. She would either spend majority of the time in her room in the computer while the TV was on, or most likely be hanging out with Lilly in her room. What would be cute and funny is that Lilly would also be in Desmarie's room for hours, while both of them just talked and relaxed together. It felt weird but super cool because it was the best of both worlds. Desmarie got to have her own room, once again. But, would have her best friend literally footsteps away under the same roof.

CHAPTER 15

This Is Not Good-Bye

Desmarie enjoyed writing poems. At the time during high school, she loved writing because it was a form of release. Sometimes what needs to be said aloud is not easy to unchain. So, writing it on paper helped and it just felt good; plain and simple as that. During new love and stupid break-ups, rumors and gossip of all types, those would end up being topics of choice to write about. One great poet that used to be out there was Rumi. He was a 13th century Persian poet and Islamic scholar. He once said, "Goodbyes are only for those who love with their eyes. Because for those who love with heart and soul, there is no such thing as separation" (Rumi, 13th century) He was spiritual, positive, and full of hope. They were similar qualities that Desmarie chose to follow and have gained to become happy during tough times in her life. She thought deeply about this as the time was getting closer to graduate and finish school. Faith followed her as she took her route. With upcoming twists and turns, never-ending curbs, she had Maria to flutter close by and keep her safe in her journey through life.

Senior prom was almost here, which was usually followed by an overnight weekend stay at the beaches in Wildwood. Desmarie was anxious but excited. It had been a long time coming and she cannot believe it was finally here. Prom was a blast, and going to wildwood afterwards would be amazing. Desmarie ended up meeting a lot of different graduates from other high schools. She ended up staying at the shore for 2 nights. The first night was at a motel close to the beach and broad walk with her good and close friends. The second night was at a friend's friend beach house that was rented out for prom weekend. The close friends' group were forced to drive back home the next day as their strict parents demanded. So Desmarie lingered off with other groups of people. Beer pong and drinks for hours on end, followed by more liquor while smoking each other out with blunts that were rolled out and ready to use from the morning. Did you know you can smoke weed through an apple? No joke! It was pretty uplifting and just plain fun to experience the sweet moment. Sitting outside the porch with a beer in hand and hearing the thrashing of the waves from far off at the beach, interrupted by the yelling and laughing from the party houses close by that were full of people.

And with that, the crazy weekend had ended, and Desmarie was driving home Sunday late morning. A little more than 3 hours during the road trip, Desmarie looked at the open road and enjoyed the wind in her face. Feeling super excited, Desmarie was anticipating her sister Babi's arrival from Miami. They both kept in contact throughout the years, especially after their mom passed. Graduation was going to be a happy but also overwhelming moment for Desmarie. Knowing what comes after, the reality of the unknown and having to figure out what she wants to do with herself was nerve-racking. Although scary, Desmarie knew that mom would always be there with her and protect her.

"Desmarie Madrid!" the principal announces into the microphone as students continue walking up to the podium to receive their diplomas. Her gold-colored graduation gown drags a bit on the ground, given the fact that Desmarie was short in height. She steps up onto the stage and the crowd goes loud again, but all of what Desmarie concentrates on hearing is her family cheering her on. Desmarie looks over to both of her sisters Lilly and Babi standing up in encouragement. She then sits down next to her fellow classmates. A breath of relief leaves Desmarie's mouth as she takes in this moment. Here we go.

From the beginning to the end of high school, Desmarie was discovering herself, who she really was and who she wants to eventually become. Many instances were befuddling, unfortunately causing some clashing with the family. But as regular teenagers come by, Desmarie was the average one. She didn't accept criticism well for the most part and she thought most of the time for herself as always right and chose not to accept advice from her parents. What added wood do the fire were also social, physical, and emotional changes to anything that was going on in those moments.

You don't know what you have until it's gone. These are the words Desmarie has lived with, and she can very well prove this saying to anyone. Be grateful for what you have, because if something close gets taken away from someone, let's say tomorrow, life will NOT be the same. It changes everything, it changes YOU. Desmarie fell into a depression state, where her body longed for something. For family. Wait, what? And also, why? She has family right here. Was it the need for more friends? No, she doesn't know really what caused that. Hormones, emotions running wild. What else is there to do in this life? Who else can she meet? Lilly was beginning to go out more and not be home more often, was that it? Desmarie had her car and she had the ability to go out as well, and she did, but something was still missing. Any moments spent alone were no help. No distraction meant being in a room with no noise and thinking. Desmarie tried to stay away from her mind as much as possible, because very frequent, her subconscious takes the lead and drives her wild with so much as to negative thoughts from everything. Why did this happen? Desmarie didn't know what to do, but she did know that she needed to leave. Maybe she needed to see her family in Florida, something that was close to her mom, familiar-like love; bonding of some sort. Things were changing, people were growing up, life was moving forward. It was time that Desmarie did the same but in a happier route that would make her better off and just happy; something to look forward to.

The decision was made with Desmarie and Ruth, and it ended up being conclusive. She was going to see her closer sister Babi who now lived in the Virgen Islands, thanks to her husband getting a promotion from his job to move over there. Maybe a getaway, a change. She also did miss her sister dearly. Oh Maria, how you are missed. Her words of wisdom, that beautiful smile that can melt an iceberg, and those warm hands that would hold Desmarie at night and cuddle together with before going to sleep. Some days were harder to get through than others. Then, it became easier as more time passed by swiftly without trauma crashing into her hearts once again and reminding them that she wasn't here anymore. With a heavy heart, Ruth agreed and thought this was the right thing to do, it was what Desmarie wanted to do at the end.

The last few weeks in New Jersey, Desmarie spent sleeping over friends' houses, she was also able to reunite with Lilly after the news broke; both of them becoming closer. Most nights, Desmarie would pack a little bit, then go out and distract herself with going to big parties that were being organized by seniors that graduated in her class of 09. Desmarie would then come home tired, and she continued packing. As the calendar days eventually flipped to the beginning of summer, it was almost time to move. July 11th, 2009 was the day. Plane ticket was purchased, a one-way flight to St. Thomas, USVI.

One of the following late nights, Desmarie left to go and pick up Lilly from a friend's house. She pulls up and honks while staying in the car. She texted Lilly to let her know that she was there. While waiting outside the mansion of a house, listening to her favorite house music, Desmarie's eyes were getting heavy. Lilly comes out the front door stumbling, opening the passenger door and giggles some words out, "What up!" Lilly could barely stay upright. As she came in the car and shut the door, she begins to recline the passenger seat. "Uhm sorry I am just sleepy and drunk," Lilly groans and starts to stare out the window since her phone was almost dead. Desmarie pulls out of the packed driveway. She carefully steers away from the giant SUV that was parked next to her for the moment, and exits the block. "Don't worry about it, are you good?" Desmarie asked Lilly to make sure she doesn't pass out to sleep right away. They come to a stop at a red light; the light at this intersection always took so long to turn green for some reason.

Desmarie was feeling so beat that she shifts into park. Luckily, there wasn't much traffic at 1 am during a week day; thank goodness for it being summer. Lilly suddenly sits up randomly and turns to Desmarie who was looking down at her phone, "Honestly no, Desmarie you can't leave because then I'll be like alone and I can't be. I am going to miss you, why are you doing this? just stay, I fucking need you to stay!" she brings her hand up briskly on top of Desmarie's shoulder, her other hand then grabs and turns Desmarie's face to look at her. "You can't leave!" as Lilly kisses her. She goes back to laying down. Desmarie lets out a small laugh while trying to get Lilly's attention to keep her awake. A few seconds pass by and the light turns green. The lingering taste of grey goose subsides on Desmarie's lips while she shifts her car into drive and drives passed the light. She placed her arm around Lilly to come closer to her and reassures her, "Don't say that, please just don't. You know very well that I will always be here for you and whenever you need me, I will literally be a phone call away. We can also iChat on our MacBook's! You are more than good here; your family is here with you and they are amazing. You will also continue to kick ass in school, right?" Desmarie asks in a soft tone knowing that Lilly wasn't acting like her entire self, right then and there. Desmarie calmly rubs Lilly's hand back and forth to help her relax. Lilly's watery eyes begin to dry, she smiles and speaks up, "I know, but you seriously do suck for doing this."

Desmarie finally arrives home. She goes to park her car in the driveway right behind Ruth's SUV while Lilly got out of the car to run inside and leave her shoes in the doorway. "Good night Lilly, see you tomorrow," Desmarie tells Lilly as she shuts the lights off the hallway. Desmarie begins to think, people have to be with someone who loves them harder on the days they can't love themselves at all. Many moments in life passed by where Desmarie didn't recognize who she was anymore, but Lilly made sure to take her by the hands and show her who she really is in this life. We are all humans and sometimes we make mistakes. But the most important thing of all is having people who love you by your side; friends who respect you and don't hurt you. Love is the most powerful of all. Love is the key to it all. Lilly was the girl that, for fuck sake, did Desmarie's hair for her senior prom! Took her shopping in the malls for pretty outfits to wear for school. Helped her fit into social groups and lessen her negative feelings of always being insecure about herself and consistently acting self-conscious about everything she does. Lilly was Desmarie's rock. Without her, truth be told, Desmarie feels like she wouldn't be standing here right now. And even if she was able to be ok without anyone by her side, she wouldn't have had the spine in her back to keep her up and standing from all of the bad that has happened to her. Lilly is an incredible girl. A true sister in which Desmarie didn't get a chance to meet until years later after being born. Blood is not thicker than water. Lilly is family. Ruth, Nick, and Duke are family. In actuality, those who hurt someone on purpose, aren't family. Desmarie hated herself for leaving them, but at the same time, she knew she had to do this. For her own better outcome, for her future, and for her independence. At least what she knows now, this is what she wants.

CHAPTER 16

The Island Life

Memories and conversations echoed in Desmarie's head from the last weeks that were in New Jersey. This was a big change that was happening. Desmarie swallowed a voluminous amount of saliva, the nerves begin to set in. The captain of the plane turned on the overhead seatbelt sign as she was coming down for a landing. Desmarie begins to feel the small turbulence and the wheels coming out from the plane to land on the ground; she looks out from her window seat. She begins to see crystal clear blue waters with aqua complexions all over, nearing the rocks and by the shore line. Astonishing views and unbelievable sights; this truly was a glimpse of what paradise looks like. "I love flying window seat," Desmarie says inaudibly while grinning to herself.

The world is full of contradictions, but our mistakes can be assets. Life goes on and we must go on as well. All Desmarie was looking forward to the most was seeing her sister Babi and giving her a giant hug. But with this, she missed Lilly. Lilly was right, their times together in New Jersey certainly flew by fast.

While waiting in baggage claim for about 15-20 minutes, Desmarie finally sees Babi from a distance. They both run up to each other and begin hugging letting out the happiest laughs. This felt so good, Desmarie began to feel the intrusive bond they both had from years ago.

Babi and her husband lived in a small 1-bedroom apartment, about 7 minutes away from their jobs. Desmarie spent her mornings going to the beach at the resort where they worked. She would have a pina colada (non-virgin of course) in one hand, and sun tan oil in the other. Her Prada sunglasses sat on the beach chair while sunbathing herself under the Caribbean sun. Man, this was the life. Listening to the calm thrashing waves of the turquoise waters in front of her. Desmarie watched and admired the water glistening upon the strong rays of the sun. She got up then took a dive into the water. Swimming underwater, she stayed for a bit with her eyes closed. She then comes back up, whipping her long hair to one side. The beaches in this island were so amazing and so beautiful. You wouldn't be able to see through the water up north; the Jersey shores were nothing like this. Miami beaches were actually similar looking in appearance but nothing compared to the actual Caribbean. This was a top destination for any vacationer around the world. This was always at the top of every travel agent's list when they consult with their clients on their next destination to travel to. It is a pricey haven, but the time spent in places like this would be well worth every penny disbursed.

Desmarie was living like royalty. She didn't have to spend any money, but she still ended up working part-time at the hotel gift shop with her sister to occupy herself and to save money. The resort where they stayed at most of the time and worked in was called Wyndham Sugar Bay, a really great and fun resort, it was also where Desmarie's brother in-law worked as director of food and beverage at the time. He was a good person to talk to for Desmarie. He gave her many pep talks with drinks always on hand, but too many of those times he would just come off as an asshole. He would irritate Desmarie about silly shit, but with good intentions at the end of the day. Babi worked at the gift shop when she first moved there, so she had a really good relationship and rapport with the hotel staff over there. Babi is really just a super fun and lovable kind of gal. It was impossible to not love her. For any nights that were open and available at the resort, Desmarie and Babi would get a room hopefully with a beach view and stay for the night. It was so much fun, the discounted rate for them three was beyond belief. The staff members at the resort were so nice and generous to Desmarie. It helped a whole lot being related to the food and beverage director and of course the lovable Babi from the store, who was also the spouse of the director for the restaurants. During the off-seasons in St. Thomas, the hotel resort would be really slow with a very small occupancy inside. Those times were actually pretty amazing since Desmarie had the beach and pool area all to herself. While living there, she met many tourists, made friends, even had a couple of her high school friends come down with their immediate families to the resort. Drinking was never limited, swimming was never limited, and funny to say that both activities were never enough in the day. This was the island life. "Every little thing gonna be all right" (Bob Marley, 1977).

Desmarie's family from New Jersey was also able to visit a couple of times. Having a blast together at the resort, they were able to share delicious types of authentic foods at the restaurants, both local and touristy; including our favorite rich and creamy pastas, mixed with super tasty meats. Of course, finishing up with scrumptious desserts. Desmarie's favorite was the Dolce dessert wine she had while visiting San Juan, Puerto Rico.

The most amazing trips taken by the two sisters were visiting the British Virgin Islands multiple times. Both Desmarie and Babi would take the ferry boat from the docks and go to Tortola, one of the British islands that would be the main place to go swimming with the dolphins, which they did several times together. "Ok, you guys are going to rehearse back to me how you are going to place and position yourself on the water, that way we can move on with the dolphins to start their tricks!" The dolphin instructor instructed the sisters plus another couple that was participating with the dolphins as well. Working with the dolphins felt like an experience of the lifetime. Swimming with these intelligent creatures was so much fun. One of Desmarie's favorite tricks was when she was doggy-paddling in the center of the salt water pool with her arms by her sides up above the water. Staying in that form, the dolphin came from behind while diving underwater, then dived upwards bringing its bottlenose as a platform underneath Desmarie's feet and rapidly carrying her up above the water to the air. So thrilling and exciting at the same time. Desmarie felt nervous in the beginning, because in general a person assumes that everything on a dolphin is wet and slippery. On the contrary, their snouts which were used to carry the sisters up above the water and thrown in the air didn't feel wet nor slippery; it felt like a small dry platform. The sisters ended their session kissing them on their nose and letting them plant a wet kiss on each one of their cheeks.

They also visited White Bay in Jost Van Dyk, arriving with their 18-foot fishing boat. Desmarie was also able to get certified in scuba diving. She took advantage of it this year when she lived with her sister. Scuba diving is truly a breathtaking experience; just imagine taking a road trip and discovering new places and locations, except you are underwater. Being underwater is like being in another world, the atmosphere down there is like something you'll never know until you experience the adventure for yourself. Being able to move in three dimensions alongside different types of fish and coral reefs, and of course while wearing state of the art diver equipment. But all kidding aside, the certification process for Desmarie was hell. Desmarie had to face and experience her fears of diving as deep as 160 ft underwater in the ocean while getting tested to take off ALL of her diving gear and equipment, then having to put it back on to wear. This scary and crazy certification process also included taking the fucking diving mask off while being underwater. So frightening and nerve racking, but she accomplished it at the end with the help and motivation of Babi being there next to her. Just thinking of all the possibilities that could be after they both got officially certified. One of them was that they wouldn't have to follow a diving instructor underwater all of the time. Once this entire torturous progression finally ended, they were able to take their boat out, park it by tying it onto a sea buoy, and free dive. Such an adventure, scary but so exciting. Isn't that how life should be? Conquering your fears and getting such an amazing award at the end?

Another great sport that Desmarie was also able to do here was jet skiing. Boy, what a rush! The days when there were strong winds, the waters became rough and Desmarie ended up waking up super sore the next day; but that was usually when starting the activity for the very first time. People ended up getting used to it after riding them many times, especially with the rough waves that would form when any storms were near. Imagine bouncing up and down, landing on a super firm seat cushion over and over again, depending how far you go out, and how fast you fight against the waves. Still, such a rush and so much fun to do!

Eventually, there would definitely be one true saying that Desmarie could share with all of you. Paradise does get tiring to be living day in and day out. Please, before you close this book and disagree with the main character, she can explain it to you! Desmarie felt coming close to a year in length, that living here in paradise felt like living a still life. In other words, not moving forward. What about college? Owning an apartment, then house? Meeting someone, meeting the one? All of that was inconclusive.

A year passed, and Desmarie was 19 years old. She desired to go to college and meeting new people her age with similar interests and hobbies. She also wanted to start up her career, whatever it was going to be. The plan was to work a lot of hours, including overtime if allowed at the gift shop, save money and then move. Desmarie always wanted to go to college in Miami; she began living there in the first place many years ago in the past before all of this anyway. Miami is like a NYC, but only with a bunch of Spanish-speaking locals walking around everywhere; something that would be familiar to her and going back to her roots. Bringing this topic up as well, her oldest sister Patty was actually living there with her husband and kids. So Desmarie wouldn't be completely by herself in a brand-new state to live in. The pattern of everyday waking up and: beach>pool>work>drink>bars>sleep> and repeat, got really tiring eventually. Not to mention, the size of the island itself was small. There were about 3 grocery stores in the entire island, one mall that was the size of maybe 5 of their 1-bedroom apartments. For the time being at nights, Desmarie didn't feel like going out really and would end up staying home. In the course of those evenings, she would stay home alone and would burn in the fire of her own thoughts;

anywhere from old negative memories and flashbacks to good and positive reminders. Desmarie fell into a darkness one night while living on the island that she stepped outside the driveway with a small knife, but her wrists refused to bleed. The main reason for that was that Desmarie couldn't build herself up to actually do it. She tried to forget that night and dismiss that negative energy that tried to enter her body once again.

Desmarie decided that she wanted to move forward with her life and start college. At the time, she was thinking to become a journalist. She enjoyed writing, and she thought maybe she can give that career path a try, kind of like Lois Lane from the Superman comics. It could be fun, and who knows, maybe she will meet a super hero that works in the desk next to hers that always wears his big goofy glasses.

Before leaving in that same year, Desmarie's niece was born in the island. The one hospital in St. Thomas had a really nice private room for her sister and the rest of her family and friends; the doctor was a pretty cool lady too. The natural and vaginal delivery from her sister went super smooth and fast. Desmarie was able to check mark off her list of fully witnessing and helping during a birth delivery. The big benefit of it all was being there for Babi at a very memorable event in her life. Her niece was born to be so beautiful; she is a true island girl.

CHAPTER 17

Welcome to Miami

"The scariest moment is always just before you start. After that, things can only get better" (Stephen King, 2002). Desmarie was moving onto the next milestone in her life. She contacted her oldest sister Patty to let her know that she was planning to move there really soon. With that news Patty went ahead and bought Desmarie a one-way ticket to Miami from St. Thomas.

All packed, Desmarie and Babi spent the last night making sure she had everything with her ready for her trip. She kept a bunch of pictures which carried a ton of memories, and of course her contact info including work number to be able to talk to each other daily. They developed a strong connection together as sisters, that neither of them wanted that to change. Babi's plan was to also move out of the island in the near future with her family; as soon as they save up some money, also when her husband gives the green light from his job and decide where to go or where to transfer. She originally wanted to be close to the family in Florida, but at the same time they also wanted change; something else rather than Miami. As luck would have it about 5 years later, they ended up moving to Texas and staying there for 3 years before returning to south Florida once again.

"Fuck I am so high right now," Lilly giggles as she takes another hit. Desmarie packed an empty bottle of water, some aluminum foil and her lighter. Lilly gave the weed to Desmarie and reclined both the passenger and driver's seat so they could both relax. The jersey sisters smoke each other out for a good hour and a half. Desmarie looked out her window as she exhaled smoke. She focused on the world within them rather than the world outside. The car windows became so foggy underneath the moonlight in the empty field at Desmarie's yard. Desmarie made sure to drive the car somewhat further away just in case, so they wouldn't get caught; they even wandered off where the Wi-Fi was weak. "Girl you are so real! I mean seriously though; you are the realest person there is that I have ever known. There is no fake piece of skin on you, you are real to the touch. You are so great to be with!" Desmarie lets out a big belly laugh as she rubs looks down to rub her eyes. "Hahaha stop it, you're too fucking funny!" Lilly glares at the car clock and lets out a quiet gasp. Realizing it was getting late, they both packed it up and drove back to the house. Desmarie laughs quietly as she experiences more flashbacks from New Jersey.

Desmarie chuckles in a soft tone of voice as she smiles while looking out her window from the plane. Daydreaming and flash-backing the fun times with family and friends is what idled her time while flying to Miami that early afternoon. Looking out to the sky, she was flying right above the Florida Keys at that moment. She begins to unfasten her seatbelt and stretch her entire body while the captain announced that it was time to land. Desmarie felt the warm and humid breeze land on top of her while she paced through the air gate tunnel into the airport; it was the month of July in 2010. "Oh, it's so hot!" Desmarie mumbles to herself as she finally gets to baggage claim. She finally sees Patty through the crowds of people waving at her. Desmarie runs while pulling her bags and goes to hug her sister.

Desmarie was accompanied by her sister to look for apartments for rent close by to where her house was located. The area she was in was super nice and quaint, a little bit more south from where their old apartment used to be with mom +10 years ago. It felt nice for Desmarie because this new area didn't appear to be familiar-looking; hence it didn't bring back memories. During 2010, prices for rent weren't that bad. At the end, after stopping at several complexes, Desmarie was successful finding a 2-bedroom 2-bath apartment for $1,098 a month for rent. Her older brother also ended up being in Miami as well, he moved back after living in Spain with dad for some time. They both decided to rent out the apartment together. Desmarie did not have a great relationship with her brother, but she thought they could both help each other and hopefully reconnect by living together.

Patty was kind enough to help Desmarie and their brother with groceries for their first week. When entering through the door into an empty apartment, Desmarie felt the stress. But it was the good kind of stress, like when you have to pack for a Disney World trip. Unpacking was the bitch. But this was Desmarie's first official apartment, and she was able to call it her own and would be able to decorate it to how she wants. Next step comes the bills and finding a job soon; god willing. Ah the real world, she knows it's going to suck but will love it regardless. Desmarie used her savings from the island to buy the furniture and wall décor for the place. It was an exciting time for her. Nights out in Miami were way too much fun. She knew that once she gets herself settled and meets new people, it would become much more fun and entertaining being here.

"My god, look at the guys here!" Desmarie's jaw slightly drops while grinning and glancing up at a tall muscular man walking by in the store; her sister laughs. The men in Miami are so physically attractive! It felt like such a different vibe here compared to living up north. First off, when you go into bars and clubs here, the guys actually dress nice, most of them even wear business casual attire; all fresh and spruced up for the evening. Desmarie wasn't sure why men up north were so different in comparison. She realized that the Latinos and Hispanics in Miami had a natural "spice" to them, both mentally and emotionally; the way they do certain things. Even the way they dance, whoa, the guys here can move their hips so well. Men here also went to the gym frequently throughout the week, it was a big deal to them. This was great. Desmarie smiles as she looks at a couple of girls that walk by passing her. "Well, I can tell you this, you will be saving about 10 grand because you do not need a boob job!" Desmarie remembers back at a funny moment between her and her brother in-law in St. Thomas. He explained to her that when she would get to Miami, she will see that almost every girl she meets will have had a boob job, Botox, or lips done. Well yeah, look around, he was completely right. One thing about Desmarie, she cared about her looks when she went out somewhere but she was never the girl to load her face up with makeup, and spend thousands of dollars to enhance anything in her body. Luckily her lips and breasts look pretty decent, she thought and wondered; no need to tweak anything. She nods in approval with a big smirk in her face when the girls exit the store in front of them.

Desmarie finally got an offer for a full-time job to start in August. She also signed up for college classes in a nearby campus to begin around the same time as well. Since she hasn't resided in Miami for a year yet, unfortunately, Desmarie had to pay triple the amount for classes due to out-of-state fees. It was silly, but Desmarie was able to do it. She attended classes part-time mostly since her job at the hospital gave her 12-hour shifts to work. She took the night shift which had more pay, but honestly, it was what they were looking for at the time so she accepted the offer since she needed to start getting money to pay her bills.

Working night shifts wasn't easy. 7pm-7am would drag at about 2-3am, kind of like the 2-3pm hour would drag in the afternoon for the average office jobs that are 9-5. It was very eventful and fun though, Desmarie got to work with really interesting and cool co-workers. The ER registration gang included very flirtatious men and gossipy women but all in all she got used to it and blended right in with the crowd. She worked for registration in the emergency room, which included entering people into the system as they came in and admitting them if needed. The chaos never stopped; you could imagine it was like the ER show that used to be on TV. This hospital job setting was making Desmarie become more interested in the healthcare field. Although trauma and anguish were witnessed regularly at the emergency room, being able to help people really appealed to her. With big trauma in her life, Desmarie knew that she would never end up becoming a nurse nor a doctor. Witnessing blood and death daily was not in her future career plans. Certain images would bring back memories; images more so into her brain, and those were not pleasant. Plenty of times, Desmarie suffered getting out of those deep thoughts but it would take minutes at a time to fully regain consciousness and alertness of what was actually around her. Yeah, it was tough in the beginning but getting distracted with everything else in her department and the comedians in her small office helped take the mind off things. It was just a registration job, dealing with the paperwork and subtracting the clinical stuff.

Desmarie would enjoy driving home early mornings and watching the beautiful sunrise while on the highway. At the same time though, she felt tired and exhausted. For about a year, she slept a good 4-5 hours at home, then would wake up and attend like 2-3 classes that same day. Some days required her to work again after those classes finished, while other days would be part of her 3 consecutive days off from the work week. It was tiring but eventually she finished all of her classes at the end of the semester and took breaks from school. Not only for convenience and comfort, but the out of state fees were also kicking her ass.

Her weekends off usually consisted of dates with guys that she would meet, usually from work. Desmarie also would hang out with friends of friends from school, usually would go out to the movies or bowling and shopping at the big malls. Those times were a lot of fun, and sometimes it would escape her mind that she had to return to work the next day and eventually school again before the year ends to have some kind of progress with classes to finish her major. But with the fun parties and times, also came the ominous moments. Desmarie at times would get stood up by a guy she was going to go out with that day or night. She would usually just blow off steam by staying home in her room with the door locked, watching TV shows. Or she would just choose to go to her sister Patty's house to hang out.

CHAPTER 18

An old friend?

The best part about being here in Miami was not being completely alone in a city that almost never sleeps. Desmarie's sister would throw fun house parties over the weekends, they were great. They would all jam to rock n' roll in the background, and there would always be a disco ball somewhere hanging since Patty is a huge 80's music fan. Her husband would usually be the bartender; over filling the drinks with way too much alcohol.

One day, Desmarie went over on a day she had off from work, and just spent time with her nephews. Someone at the front door begins to knock, Patty goes to see who it is. When the door opened, a tall, dark-skinned dude came in smiling and went to greet the family. Desmarie wasn't sure who that was, she stayed in the living room but stood up from the couch to go meet him. "Hey I am Desmonte, I went to school with your brother, well just the senior year of high school," he shook Desmarie's hand in a friendly matter while smiling at her. Desmarie giggled, "Oh wow, I am surprised I never met you officially! Maybe we did meet years ago and I just can't remember." There was a perfectly good explanation as to why these 2 didn't meet before. Desmarie did move up north when she was about to turn 10 years old, so it makes sense that she didn't catch him; she rarely saw her siblings nor spent time with them as it is. "Crazy, I didn't know you had a little sister

Patty," Desmonte glances over to Desmarie again, then looks back to Patty and continues the conversation. In several times, Desmarie caught Desmonte glimpsing at her. Eventually, they both exchanged numbers and became friends quickly.

Desmonte was living in Tampa Bay, FL at the time. He would visit his friends (Desmarie's siblings) maybe 2-3 times a year for a little while now, but this year it became a little bit different. He would be driving down like once a month to visit, more frequent compared to previous times. It was a 3 ½ hour drive and he treated it like nothing. Got to give it to him, driving those hours intermittently isn't easy. Maybe there was a reason why the visits ended up being periodically lately.

Desmonte developed feelings for Desmarie. They would all get together at Patty's house parties like every other weekend, when she had her weekends off from work. It was nice of them all to make the big plans around the days Desmarie didn't have to work, after all, the get-togethers weren't as fun without her. Desmarie lived in Miami and took advantage of the single life. She and Desmonte would be seen flirting in many instances, however, feelings were not mutual. Although Desmarie enjoyed his company, she didn't feel the same way he felt for her. Like mentioned before, Desmarie enjoyed being single and dating cute guys; sad to say most of them were idiots at the end. Why is it always the case that it is so easily to fall for the jerks? The men that treat you like shit? Luckily, Desmarie kept it casual and didn't get into anything serious. Even if she wanted to, one of them would end up ghosting the other most of the time, or just lose interest.

A little more than a year finally passed living in Miami. Desmarie registered once again for some classes since she was able to pay less for them now. Things back at the apartment weren't going so well. Desmarie's brother continued to not pay his half of the rent that was due every month. She would let this go a lot of times in that year, but it reached the point where she was over the bullshit. She still dealt with it because the apartment was under a year lease, and like mentioned before, the plan when all of this started was family helping other family out, right? Well, her brother ended up being a deadbeat to conclude all of this. There was even one instance where one of them almost left the apartment, but it didn't happen. It was about to be summer, and Desmarie wasn't sure what she was going to do. She had thoughts cross her mind daily on maybe moving to a 1-bedroom apartment, but honestly speaking, she enjoyed not living alone. She enjoyed company; we've known this for a long time. Times alone don't go well for her; Desmarie ended up sitting down and just thought about it. What was she going to do?

Even though this was happening at home, the siblings still got together frequently at their sister's place and even went downtown multiple times; one time specifically to a Miami Heat game. It was an away game, so they all went to the American Airlines Arena to watch it virtually in an empty stadium. It was kind of weird but pretty cool at the same time. Desmarie's brother begins to nag her and let her know that Desmonte appeared to be completely over her as he was seeing and/or being heard that he was dating around. While bothering and teasing Desmarie, her brother was also occupied typing on his phone. For odd reasons, this bothered Desmarie. Not only has she been getting more and more angry with her brother, to add this frustration to the list wasn't going to be great; little did we know, it would push her over the edge. Why? It's not like she has feelings for Desmonte, right? Didn't we clear that up earlier in the chapter? Well, Desmarie took his phone in a nasty and brisk matter, saw a text image, then flung it back to her brother. She then took her iPhone out and began texting: "You know this is complete bullshit, you think you are so great and can date anyone and just be whatever about it... ..," Desmarie kept rambling on mentioning that this coming from her is unnecessary and foolish and just typing things that in reality didn't go together but what we can all say is she was upset. Desmarie was heated while typing, she sits back down from standing the whole time and watches the game as she puts her phone away into her pocket. Seconds later, she takes it back out. Her phone vibrates minutes later as it goes off more than once; receiving more than one incoming text message. "You know what you need to get off your high horse, who do you think you are telling me" ...it goes on and on,

Desmarie continues to read angrily at what Desmonte typed to her. She wasn't feeling confused, she just knew she was angry, period.

After the game was over, her brother in-law drove them back home. A couple of weeks pass, Desmarie and Desmonte were still on unspeaking terms. Desmarie went out on her days off and spent it being with friends, as well as drinking. Still upset at the current situation, she didn't let it affect her, or so she thought.

An event happened one night, where something happened at the right time and place. It was something very shitty, but at the end, played a huge part and a necessary role as to where we all are now. Desmarie took her bathing suit out from her dresser, then went to Patty's house to go night swimming. Her brother in-law set up a beer pong table outside in the yard and played with Desmarie and her brother while blasting their favorite rock music in the background. Desmarie gets out of the pool minutes after going in, and puts her hoodie and pants back on. She was seen texting, then putting her phone away in her front sweatshirt pocket, and took it out again. She went to get a drink really quick and starts walking back next to the pool. Both her brother and brother in-law, looking right at her, caused an element of surprise where they ended up running up to her and pushed her into the pool. Of course, this happened so fast that Desmarie didn't even have the seconds of time to react and yell at both of them to let them know her phone was in her pocket. Splash! Desmarie comes up from underwater quickly and tosses her phone to the edge of the pool. An iPhone, soaking wet, lying there in front of Desmarie's shocked expressive look on her face. She quickly glances at both guys, "Are you fucking kidding me? Why would you fucking do that!" Desmarie gets to her brother's face furiously and continues yelling at him. "I didn't know you had your phone, chill!" her brother tries to calm her in the most careless way possible. Desmarie's sister comes outside quickly to find out what the commotion was about. Looking at her husband in disbelief, she runs back inside and takes Desmarie's phone with her. She placed it in a small bowl of dry, raw rice. Supposedly this helps to soak up any water and/or moisture from the phone, but Desmarie already felt hopeless. Tears begin streaming down her face as she continues to shout angrily at everyone. About 20 minutes pass by, but nothing. Her phone still doesn't work. Nobody says anything in the room, except Patty who kept consoling Desmarie. Her brother in-law marches quickly up the stairs, then comes back downstairs and hands Desmarie a check of $100.00. "Here is half for the damage, I am so sorry," her brother in-law apologizes showing regret in his face. Desmarie takes the check and just weeps. Waiting on her brother to say something or maybe attempt to give her some money for the fucking trouble he caused, but no. Come on, we are all talking about a guy that hasn't made his part of the rent for like half the year; it's all a fucking joke. Not offering Desmarie any financial help to replace her broken phone, nor even apologizing to her, Desmarie had the last straw with him. That's the fault in us, why do we look for sympathy in the wrong places, from the wrong people? Desmarie felt like she was at a funeral that night, sobbing over a phone for goodness sake! But, nowadays in this new decade, everybody has their life on their phone. Unfortunately, Desmarie just lost all of her info that was saved onto her iPhone to a stupid accident.

About a week passed and Desmarie was able to get going with buying a new replacement iPhone. Not downgrading because once someone owns a smartphone like that, it is impossible to downgrade to a different phone. News traveled fast, and Desmonte heard what happened through her sister Patty. Desmonte felt bad at the situation, thinking about and also knowing how important Desmarie's phone was to her. Keeping the same phone number of course, Desmarie's phone begins to go off. It was a text alert from Desmonte. "I am sorry for what happened, your sister told me everything. Your brother is such a jerk, sorry you had to go through that. Were you able to fix it, or replace it?" Desmarie reads the text message twice and a smile forms on her face. She was glad that he reached out to her, and she felt better. Desmonte was kind enough to always look out for her and make sure everything was ok. He was always so sincere and kind to her. Desmarie was just your ordinary blind 20-year-old (metaphorically speaking), who doesn't know nor realize that the perfect guy for her is right there in front of her face; Desmonte.

CHAPTER 19

Roommates

Desmonte ended up leaving his place in Tampa Bay, and moved down to Miami since he really had nothing left up north. He had broken off with his ex-girlfriend sometime before living by himself without roommates. He came down to live at his dad's house who lived about 5 minutes away from Desmarie's apartment. He ended up living there for about 6 months. Desmarie would go over his house and hang out to watch shows and movies and just talk to him. She would be her normal flirty self. They both also ended up kissing after coming home from house parties, drunk. Blame it on the alcohol. Right? During other fun festivities together, they both would get home late at night and fool around some more but it never led up to "the thing". They weren't going out, and to be clear, Desmonte lived his life while Desmarie lived hers so no feelings changed; or did they? In the prior year, Desmarie turned him down when he asked her out. Desmarie told him that she didn't have the same feelings for him as he did for her; she considered him to be a good friend. Although those moments happened, both of them did still enjoy their times spent together.

One of the many days where Desmarie went over to Desmonte's house, they picked out a movie to watch in the living room. Looking through the kitchen cabinets for popcorn, Desmonte had no luck. Thinking for a little, he ended up making a plate of bacon as a movie snack. Desmarie began to smell the bacon and laugh, "Oh my goodness, what a great idea! We are such fat asses!" Desmarie exclaims while she continued roaring with laughter. Not declining the idea, she sat down next to Desmonte on the sofa with the plate of bacon and played the movie. These were days where Desmarie was her happiest. She didn't feel stress from home because she wasn't there, nor work. Just spending time with a good friend being silly together was enough for her.

Desmarie one early morning was driving home from work, it was a rough night in the ER and she was over it. She was talking with Desmonte over the phone letting him know how stressed she felt living with her brother. After finishing work, she never looked forward to coming home because she would have to see him. Desmonte invited her over to talk in person better, so he can better understand the situation. "You know what though, why don't you move in with me? I am literally about to kick my brother out because he hasn't paid his part of the rent for like half the year, there is no point in having him as a roommate anymore. I already spoke with him, so you should talk with him and make it work," Desmarie explained to him and hoping he would like the idea. Desmonte at the end agreed to it and decided to help Desmarie out with the current living status. He later reached out to Desmarie's brother and reasoned with him about what is better for him to do.

Desmonte finished up packing and grabbed his last bag to put in his car. He drove to Desmarie's place and parked out in the front. "Hey!" Desmarie yells out from the outside hallway and goes to give Desmonte a hug. She was cleaning and picking up her place since her brother didn't clean nor tidy up anything when he moved out. Both Desmarie and Desmonte ended up straightening up the place to make it look more decent and better than before.

After the move, the rest of the year felt like it had flown by. Desmarie had helped Desmonte get a job in the hospital where she was working at earlier in the year when he was staying with his dad. He was able to get the afternoon shift while Desmarie stayed working the nights. She eventually accepted an afternoon shift that became available after a few months that passed by. It was nice living with Desmonte. Unlike any other guy that Desmarie had known, he was responsible and even knew how to cook many different types of food. He cleaned up after himself and knew how to organize certain things in their place really nice. Desmarie felt glad that he ended up moving in with her. Part of her was afraid he was going to decline the offer; she wasn't sure why in the moment but she just felt a little guilty. Desmonte is such a compassionate guy and to be fair, she was a lucky girl to have him there.

A few months later a trip came up where Desmarie's parents got her a plane ticket to go to Cancun with them. This was actually the second time they all went as a family to Cancun, Mexico. The first trip was a year ago in 2010 when they all went for a friend's wedding. This time around, it was for Lilly's sweet 16 celebration. Man, what a birthday bash! Traveling to a destination in Cancun ends up being an amazing time for any party-goer. It's easy to get away with drinking when you're younger than 18; especially when you are part of a large group of people. The family went to a famous club called Coco Bongo; the club seen in the classic Jim Carey movie The Mask. The night began with drinks in hand, then shots. At about 11:30pm, the music finally changes from the local choices. "Let it Rain on Me" by Pitbull featuring Marc Anthony came on, and the smoke with colorful laser lights come out of the machine behind the DJ playing that night. Desmarie, Lilly, and her friends go wild and they all climb on top of the bar. In the club Coco Bongo, there would be times during the late evening where the bartenders would clear the tables and let you dance on top. When this hit song came on, the club began to get crazy. Smoke filled the entire room as the sisters and the rest of the group danced on the bar. The girls formed a conga line where in each corner of the bar, there was a bartender tilting each person's chin up to pour tequila shots in their mouths. It was an insane amount of fun that night. The tequila down there was nothing like the states. It tasted so much better and went down way smoother compared to the other brands they were used to back home. Relaxing their minds and continuing to grind, the girls had a great time that night. After midnight, the girls got back to their hotel room and blew up a beer pong floaty for the pool. Since each room of the resort had its own small pool overlooking the huge resort, the friends took advantage and hung out outside after getting home from wherever they went to those evenings. Their fridge would be packed with Coronitas beer daily by room service; almost all of them would be done after midnight came along.

Desmarie had such an amazing time in Cancun. The group had also gone dirt biking and quadding up the hills of Mexico, zip lining into underground caves and springs, and drank tequila at local tiki huts that were in the middle of nowhere next to the roads. They also went out to other clubs those nights; with the girls dressing to impress.

After the week ended, Desmarie flew back home feeling calm and relaxed knowing she was coming back to a non-stressful home; where she no longer had to deal with an uncomfortable environment. Desmarie would talk to her family on occasion on how things were going and just catch up on all of the stuff happening. Ruth would always mention to Desmarie that the perfect guy for her to be with was living with her under the same roof. There was actually this one day where it stuck to Desmarie's mind always. The time of the month came around and Desmarie wasn't feeling too good. Hearing and knowing about this from texting her, Desmonte dropped off a sub sandwich from Publix with a box of Midol and toilet paper on her front door. Another day, Desmarie had a bad day due to fighting with Lilly over the phone over some plagiarism shit in school. She came home to a bouquet of flowers that night, also with a box of chocolates sitting on her nightstand in her room. Desmarie knew that Desmonte was a really good guy, but the feelings just weren't mutual on her end. It's not like she can force her feelings to change overnight. Her best friend Lilly would pester her as well and also threatened playfully that if Desmarie didn't marry him, that she was going to so he doesn't get away. They laughed that off during a Miami visit where Lilly visited Desmarie and stayed with them for about a week or so.

Desmarie was looking forward to her 21st birthday that was coming up in a month; it was April, 2012 at the time. She was taking some classes at the college nearby, using Desmonte's car to drive there and back on days that he was off from work. Desmarie unfortunately got into a car accident earlier that year. Remembering it now, the event was scary. Desmarie was driving home one night in the pouring rain. About to get off her exit, she sees from a small distance away a car spinning out of control in the middle of the 4 lanes. Without much control but fully aware of the situation, she didn't want to stop short or drastically change lanes because she didn't know if there were cars behind her. With having no time to check, she reacted quickly and slowly veered to the right but didn't realize that the other car was gliding fast to her side because of the wet tires. The car kept spinning and ended up crashing to the left side of Desmarie's car, striking the driver's door and damaging part of the back seat on the left rear. Desmarie got out of her car with fury. She felt foolish and angry at the other driver, not knowing really as to why he lost control. Of course, she wondered what if she had switched multiple lanes quickly? Would she have gotten hit by another car maybe? She couldn't take the chance. In all honestly, as with any other car accident, it happened so fast with not having enough time to think and analyze what to do; let alone react to it. Desmarie wanted to be safe; even if it meant for a chance to possibly get hit; just a quick impulse. Welp, there was no way to turn back time and change what just happened. Desmarie got into a car accident. "Fuck! ugh come on Desmonte pick up," Desmarie was dialing Desmonte's phone. "Desmonte, hey you have to come here, I got into a car accident, please just come!" Desmarie urged Desmonte while shaking. Desmarie was seen shivering due to her nerves and also being soaking wet from the rain. The younger guy that hit her was still wearing his work uniform; he was some kind of cook at a restaurant. "Hey, don't worry about it, I'll call my insurance, in the meantime just come with us and we can take you to the hospital just in case," the young man alerted and told Desmarie. She thought about it but was still on the phone with Desmonte. "Desmarie, I hear that guy in the background. Don't go with him, don't even leave from there, I am coming now to get you," Desmonte sounded aggressive but calm. He left the apartment and went into his car. "Ok, no problem just hurry!" Desmarie confirmed with Desmonte that she was going to wait there but be inside her car. The police finally arrived at the scene.

They wrote up the report as to what each one of them said. The report at the end, when it was submitted to the insurance companies, came up being pretty inaccurate as to the what had actually happened in the car accident. Reading that report caused the auto insurances to believe that it was Desmarie's fault at 100%. Luckily when the final steps were taken, Desmonte helped her out with talking to her insurance company and Desmarie ended up having to pay 15% of the damage; much better than 100% at least. Thank goodness for Desmonte being here.

One of the afternoons later that week, both Desmonte and Desmarie went together in his Mitsubishi to pick up Desmarie's Corolla at the shop. He did her the favor so that he can be with her just in case she needed him for any questions or concerns they give to her at the repair shop. Everything ended being ok and Desmarie had to spend close to $2,000 for her car. Driving back home, Desmarie stopped right behind Desmonte at a red light. She suddenly began to realize and think, "Hm, he went with me to pick up my car, he helped me keep my attendance up while I was able to show up to my classes after that stupid accident. He is there for me at any time I need him. Huh, I am looking at him driving in front of me, I see the shape of his head full of black hair right in front of the driver's seat. I want to be in there with him, I want to be there sitting next to him." Thoughts continued rolling into Desmarie's head. She continued to be deep in thought for the rest of the ride home. What is this strange feeling that she was suddenly feeling?

Coming towards the end of the month, Desmonte and Desmarie took a trip to this amazing winery about a half hour away from their place. The winery is known for their tropical fruity wines and wine tasting. Both of them went over the weekend while spring was still upon them, and took a tour of the winery. They walked through the brewery process tour as well since the place also sold beers from local distilleries. It ended up being a really good day for the friends. Days like these, Desmarie has always remembered every detail and emotion felt during those moments. It meant a great deal for her and she felt good and comfortable. Best of all, she feels like being by Desmonte makes her a more patient and unselfish person; a better person somehow.

Both of them came home that day late in the afternoon, buzzed with wine flowing all over their bloodstream. They fooled around while also sharing a long intimate kiss that night before going to sleep. Both of them watched TV at the end in their rooms. It was a good day and to be clear, they are just friends.

CHAPTER 20

Hello Love, Nice to Meet You

May 15th finally came into play though it actually landed on a Tuesday, so Desmarie's party plans were going to be moved to the weekend after; obviously since she will finally be at age to drink. Her sister Patty helped plan out where to go and which sports bars/clubs were good enough to celebrate a 21st birthday celebration. Desmarie ended up picking a really neat Irish pub located at the heart of Miami by downtown. Desmarie invited pretty much everyone she worked with, assuming not everyone was going to make it. But she was wrong, how could she assume such things when locals usually don't miss out on a night like this having this type of celebration take place? All of her co-workers and other people from the ER department at her hospital job showed up, including of course her sister and brother in-law. Desmonte left work at around 11pm and came straight from there. A couple of other good friends carpooled to the bar as well. What a night! By 10pm, Desmarie was done. She didn't voluntarily get to the point of full out drunkenness on her own, we can all blame it on her friends who kept buying her shot after shot. She wasn't going to rudely deny a drink.

Desmonte drove Desmarie's car home with Desmarie reclined in the passenger seat. The radio was playing house music, in which Desmarie tried to stay up to enjoy it. In the middle of driving in the somewhat busy highway, Desmonte looks over and notices Desmarie open the car door to throw up. "Ohhh I am sorry I didn't want to get my car dirty!" Desmarie slurs her speech as she reclines back again. Desmonte looks ahead and tries to ignore his heart racing to what had just happened. They both get home and Desmarie takes off her dress to put on pajama pants and a shirt. She then lays down and crashes onto her bed. Desmonte went to take off her heels and placed them in her bathroom since they had a little bit of throw up on top. He then took off his tie and shoes and laid down next to her. He wanted to stay with her for the night to make sure she doesn't roll on her back and God forbid vomits again.

The sun rises early the next day, Desmonte woke up early and left Desmarie's room making sure she stayed fine. Desmarie finally wakes up late morning around 11:30am, hungover as shit but felt ok overall. She took her phone and was on her social media for a while posting up pictures from last night. She smiled big as she swiped through all of the pictures taken, everyone had a blast thankfully.

Almost 2 months after her 21st celebration, Desmarie was finally able to start working the afternoon shift. She had finished her classes by Spring semester, so she was feeling good and accomplished. During one of her work days, she was assigned to work in the pediatric department. It was about 10:15pm, 45 minutes remaining until her shift was over. That day, July 13, was confusing, and Desmarie spent most of it somewhere else (mentally). For some reason, she kept thinking about Desmonte. The communication that day wasn't the usual "hey, how are you, ok see you later" texting window. The messages to each other were more attentive and sounded more thoughtful compared to anytime else ever. Desmarie was texting him and asking what he was doing, why blah blah, oh and how blah blah; blabbering about random topics just because she wanted to talk with him. It made her day go by quicker, that was usually the case any other work day. They both spoke to each other a lot when they weren't both home at the same time. The difference this time was, Desmarie noticed her eyes grew wider and more opened as to what was going on lately. "Wait a second, why am I being like this? Haha I can't stop texting him, I don't really...want to." Desmarie was realizing that she started to have feelings for Desmonte. "Shit, shit! this is really happening, oh my god, this is happening." Desmarie felt excited but also nervous, she planned out mentally what she was going to do that night. She texted Desmonte again in that hour slot, letting him know that she wants to talk to him about something, to please stay up just in case until she gets home. Desmonte nodded on the other side of the phone but texted her saying ok and that he will see her soon.

Desmarie comes home to the smell of chicken and rice being cooked. There were many nights where Desmonte would cook for her on days she would go to work and he was off. Desmarie goes to greet him while walking to her room to put her stuff down. She then walks back into the kitchen and goes to the refrigerator door. Desmarie opens the door, but after 4 seconds pass, she closes it again. She looks over to Desmonte and speaks softly, "Hey, look I have been feeling this all day, and honestly I don't know, I think I have feelings for you. Might have been maybe more than a day and I just didn't realize it, but I don't know. I feel this now and I wanted to ask you. I wanted to ask you out." Desmarie notices her hands getting cold because she felt nervous. She spilled the truth out, knowing that it can go one or two ways. Desmonte can say yes and they can officially be together as a couple. Or, it can go to shit and he can say, well, no. "Oh my god, finally!" Desmonte puts his phone down and goes to hug and kiss Desmarie. After a long passionate kiss, they both look at each other and smile. Desmarie giggles in a cute matter and caresses his left cheek. She goes in for another kiss but Desmonte quickly leaves the room and heads to his bedroom and sits in front of his desktop computer. Desmarie follows right after him and asks, "What are you doing?" Desmonte goes to the Facebook home page to sign in. "I have to update my status, duh!" Desmonte is seen still grinning and clicking away until that part was completed and the page refreshed. "There you go," Desmonte points to the screen. Desmarie takes a peek at it and sees "in a relationship with Desmarie Madrid". Desmarie laughs gratefully and goes to kiss him again while putting her arms around him.

The kiss becomes more intimate as both of them stumble over to the foot of the bed. Desmarie starts to breathe heavier as Desmonte begins to kiss her neck. Eyes closed, all Desmarie was able to see or feel was happiness. This feels so good, this feels so right. This feels like…we should have been doing this for a while. Thoughts of desire continue to cloud her mind as Desmonte nudges her onto the bed. Laying on her back, she looks at him, he looks back at her. They both stare and smile at each other intensively. Those dark yet light honey eyes, pools of ink, devouring the light in the intensity that surrounds both of them now. The appearance of a brown sunset and jet in their depth, Desmarie continues to be drawn to Desmonte's eyes looking straight at her. She winks at them, then looks down to kiss his hairless chest; she loves that. When he glanced at her again, she felt those nebulous eyes reflect the heavens. She finally knows now what it means to gaze upon the stars up close; Desmarie gives in to love. All of this was way overdue.

The night was long with romance. This was where Desmarie wanted to be. She loved being in his room, lying next to him while stroking his abdomen and giggling about random things spoken with him. He is unlike any other guy Desmarie has ever met. He wasn't into sports nor did he have the desire to go out to bars and drink constantly. Desmonte didn't fancy drinking it up every weekend neither. He would also always be good couching it at night, binging on shows or watching movies, or maybe both. There were so many qualities that Desmarie little by little fell in love with without realizing. She feels that she liked him before this day finally came, but the problem was that she didn't realize it; she was blind and oblivious to what was in front of her and what she was actually feeling. But why didn't she realize it? It's unknown because sometimes we don't know why certain things don't happen at certain times. Maybe it wouldn't have been right at the time. This felt very much like it was meant to be now. Also, to put things plain and simple, Desmarie was just overall a foolish girl. Like many girls out there, you know who you are, she would prefer to be easily attracted to the jerks in the city. She would spend many nights having a blast, also experienced a one-night stand, to later that same evening leaving each other and then back to being alone. No closeness, no connection. So many nights were spent crying on top of her bed alone. Emotions are hard, but that's why you come out stronger at the end. And it was furthermore that she would hear it weekly from her mom Ruth over the phone, asking Desmarie what exactly she was waiting for, why she wasn't closing the gap. This relationship had a fanbase, funny to say, with many people rooting for the couple to finally get together, while others just advised in the sidelines to give it up and move on. Thankfully, Desmonte didn't move on completely. Lucky enough for Desmarie, she proved her liking to him when he faked a date to Dave and Busters one night with another girl during the spring that same year. Desmonte never mentioned to Desmarie yet that he actually lied about that, wanting to see how she would react to him saying that. Desmarie showed her jealousy by accident, made it super obvious and got upset that night. Right there at that moment was when Desmonte realized that he was not going to give up on her; he just might have a chance still with her. Thank goodness for that! When you finally find the person to love, you will begin to think and realize why it was so worth the wait.

Desmonte and Desmarie spent many nights sleeping together in his room. But with less sleep recently nowadays, she realized that sleep was no longer a means of escape. She always wants him; she always wanted him, even when she didn't know what she wanted, even before knowing who he was to her. Desmarie knew that Desmonte existed, but she didn't know him personally. In the future someday, she knew she would be extremely thankful for every guy that had broken her, because it would be the reason that she has the right love now. The fun times they spent with each other are completely effortless. The euphoria displayed in public was obvious, and even in pictures that were taken of both of them, they would look like they just made sense together. Desmarie always mentioned to Desmonte that she remembers seeing him in old younger photos with her brother and sisters but he would never be seen smiling at the camera. After those times, he was still always serious in snapshots, until him and Desmarie got together. His feelings for her have been inconceivable, her feelings for him were unmasked. Desmonte is really the entire package. Desmarie feels so blessed, and just wonders that maybe everything that has happened in her life, tragic or not, led up to this. With bad comes a lot of good. This happening right here was well worth it. This was going to be her life, and she was interested in being fully on board. Looking back through memories of the past, Desmarie realizes that she regrets nothing. Everything pointed the way to this, and both Desmarie and Desmonte were so excited to pursue each other together from there on.

A week and a day after that amazing day had passed, Desmonte planned their first official date night that following Saturday. He took Desmarie out to dinner to the Melting Pot restaurant. The Melting Pot is a fondue restaurant with different and unique types of food entrees. It was both of their first times dining there and it ended up being so memorable and lovely at the same time. Desmonte and Desmarie ate breads with different kinds of cheese fondues in the beginning for their appetizer, then steak and seafood entrees that they both cooked in front of each other. And finally, a yummy dessert called Ying Yang which was a mix of chocolate and white chocolate fondue created together in a pot. They dipped different types of fruits in there, along with pieces of rice krispies that the waiter served to them. Desmonte looked at Desmarie while taking his drink. She looks back and smiles. Those sweet and dark chocolate eyes sunk into Desmarie's vision as they continued eating. He shifted his body closer to Desmarie since they were both sitting on a booth. He lifted her chin up with a soft and gentle touch and stared deep into the windows of her soul. Desmarie let out a soft and tender chuckle, thinking to herself how funny it is that so many girls fall for guys that have blue eyes. But the truth is, she wouldn't change Desmonte's brown eyes for anything else. The specs of glowing stolen sunlight in his eyes continued looking at Desmarie; they truly do make the night stars jealous. She didn't wish for ocean blue eyes for him, those would drown her. Desmarie smiles deeply as she sinks into Desmonte's arms.

The couple talked for hours at the restaurant while drinking their glasses of Paso Robles red wine. The bottle went gradually quick as they continued laughing with an infinite number of kisses being drawn in between. Their food was being heard in the background sizzling in the pot of oil, small droplets splatter out as the couple put more pieces of meat in to cook. Apparently making a romantic show to an audience, a man with a suit that worked there went up to their table and asked how their service was with them. "How are you doing this evening, is the food to your liking?" the gentleman asked politely. "Yes, very much! Thank you, everything was really great," Desmonte said to the restaurant worker. The worker speaks again while looking at the couple, "Are you celebrating a wedding anniversary?" Desmarie smiles looking at Desmonte and giggles in a pleasant manner while turning her head to the worker, "Oh no, this is the first date." Desmonte releases a big smirk while looking at Desmarie, He puts his arm around her with confidence. "Whoa, a first date!" the restaurant worker was looking over to Desmarie. "I wonder what he will be doing for you when your wedding anniversary comes up, or birthday, imagine!" he was astonished while showing inclination that he will be seeing the couple again soon in the future. While the worker was turning to pour more wine into their glasses, Desmarie sees his name tag and sees "Manager" as the title underneath his name. He shares a farewell to the lovely couple while walking away. Desmarie felt so flattered during that moment. She felt like complete royalty, never has she experienced a date like this. It was also incredible that another employee walked over to their table later that night and asked them how the everything was going. Wow, Desmonte is such a real man, Desmarie admires how well he treats her; so respectful. He knows exactly how to treat people; better yet how to treat a woman. Men at Desmarie's age shouldn't even be considered as men. They are more like children, or immature boys. Desmarie felt secure around Desmonte, she enjoyed every occasion with him.

CHAPTER 21

I Can't Say it Enough-
I Love You More
Than Anything

Trips have been taken to all over northern parts of Florida throughout the following months. Disney World makes it to the top 10 of the favorite's lists, as well as Sanibel Island in the mid-western region of Florida. Sanibel had multiple shell beaches and wildlife refuges that were so intriguing to visit and see. The sand reminded Desmarie of the Caribbean, white like thin flour and super soft to the touch. When picking it up, it slowly cascades down in between the fingers. The beaches were mesmerizing and so gorgeous there. One of the greatest things about this trip was that they made it there during off-season, so beaches were almost empty and wildlife refuges were deserted. No lines of people to wait for to do any outdoor activity over there. It felt nice to get away from Miami traffic and people; being in the presence of constant rush hour noise anywhere you go or visit is sometimes exhausting. Even an hour drive away to somewhere else felt like a vacation.

Disney trips are always so amazing. Since she was little, Desmarie has perpetually been so in love with anything that has to do with Disney.

It was thanks to her sister Babi who got her into the magical world that is Disney. All of the movies and games were great, and going to Orlando was a blast every time. You get to be a little big kid when you are there, with society and the environment being so welcoming and nice to their guests. "Have a magical day!" is just one of the many things the employees yell out to you when you leave a store or your hotel resort. The Disney world resorts are so incredibly beautiful form inside and out. When Desmonte and Desmarie stay there, they get benefits of having extra hours in any park visited. With an endless number of perks that anyone has a chance to get when going there, makes every dollar spent worth it. Desmonte and Desmarie made multiple trips there just the two of them, also some trips with his brothers and friends as well. One Halloween, they were able to attend Halloween Horror Nights, at Universal Studios, which was so fantastic. Desmarie has been to Universal Studios maybe twice in her whole life, so that was pretty cool for her.

In Desmonte and Desmarie's first trip to Disney together, they stayed at Westgate Resort in Orlando. She remembers the best part of that cozy room was the hot tub. One of the most amazing things to do was of course getting to the parks at like 8am, super early. Spend the entire day either there or park hop to another Disney park, then head back to the hotel and just soak their feet and bodies in the tub for an hour or two. With all of the walking everyone does when they go to Disney, what this couple can recommend for vacationers is to get a hotel room with either a big long tub or even a deep soaking tub, to recover from the walks. That will literally rejuvenate you and make you feel amazing. It would help alleviate your feet which are realistically used the entire day to bear your full body weight when walking the parks. Each time Desmarie and Desmonte went to Disney together, they would try to upgrade their stay, also depending how long they were staying there for. But to be honest, Westgate Resort was only once, since it wasn't a Disney resort. Once the couple spoke to a close friend that works with a travel agent for his trips, they discovered that anyone can benefit a lot more with staying at a Disney resort.

Besides traveling together as time went on, Desmonte and Desmarie also ended up buying a puppy from a store near their home. This was on their minds for the entire year as it was a big step for them, but when going to animal shelters, there was just no connection made with any of the dogs that were there sadly. Feeling bad, they would both go back home and not try to look for months later. Within a month, they stopped at a pet store near home across from a Walmart store and saw a cute little Jack Russell Terrier puppy by the window looking at the cash register in the front. My god was she cute, she didn't stop looking at Desmarie. Then once she glanced at Desmonte, it was over; he fell in love. She was it, they had to take her. Not having enough money at the very moment in their wallets, they both put a hold on the puppy just in case so they can pay the rest of the balance the end of that week or the next but also not to worry about someone else claiming her. The couple got home and within a couple of hours of discussion, planning and thinking, Desmarie gets up from the sofa and grabs her car keys to go back to the pet shop with Desmonte.

It's nice to have a puppy at home. Someone to greet you when you get home from anywhere else. Of course, having no perception of time, puppies/dogs can't tell if their owner has been gone 5 hours or 5 minutes. It all feels like 5+ hours, too long for them. It's cute but you also sometimes feel bad for them; especially being stuck working long hour shifts at a job.

The following summer, the happy couple took a trip to New Jersey to attend Desmarie's brother Duke's wedding. It was so nice to see the family again, and this time, with her amazing boyfriend by her side. Desmarie couldn't wait to show him off, especially to her family, the people that have raised Desmarie the best. Ruth and Nick ended up falling in love with Desmonte. The family in New Jersey, including all of the cousins and distant relatives in New York, accepted Desmonte to the family; they really loved meeting him. It was such an amazing trip, and such a fun and beautiful wedding ceremony and reception. The weather ended up being clear skies with the sun shining, perfect weather for a wedding. The bride's dress was stunning, and Duke looked so handsome in his tux. When the married couple came out in celebration after the church service, Desmarie clapped loudly with watery eyes being visible to the people around her. She loved Duke like a brother, he really cared for her all of those years. Desmarie reminisced about when Ruth told her what Duke did for her, how he went to talk to Victor when all of that shit was happening where Desmarie was getting kicked out of her own house by Victor's granddaughter. He is such an amazing person and brother to her, now getting married to a beautiful bride. She was another lucky person to be added to this wonderful family. Little did Desmarie know, that a day before Duke's wedding, Desmonte had spoken to Nick in the kitchen, while Desmarie was in the bedroom talking to Ruth. He asked Nick for his blessing to marry his second daughter. Nick responded, "Are you sure you don't want to ask Victor instead?" Desmonte clarified, "No, Desmarie always mentioned you as her dad and always called you Dad." Nick without hesitation let out a big, warm smile and gave Desmonte a firm handshake. He granted his blessing.

CHAPTER 22

Super Heroes Are Real

Desmonte's favorite super hero is Batman. And funny enough, Desmarie always had a thing for catwoman as she was smart, sneaky, and sexy. She always made a big impact on whoever she met. But Batman, he is one of a kind. From the all of the loss he dealt with in his life, he became stronger as each day passed. To be quite honest, it's surprising that he ended up not becoming a killer. He was able to become a hero to the people; despite the hell he went through. How did he escape the darkness? Or did the darkness help him? He remained fearless and symbolic to his audience. Also was an expert tactician and of course, just because you had a dark past, doesn't necessarily mean you become evil. Look at Desmarie, ended up having a blessed upbringing, but let's not forget her past was painful and something she will never forget.

Desmonte is Desmarie's super hero. He is patient, strong, brave, and caring. He protects her and loves her like no other. Guys in the past that wanted Desmarie never really flattered her to the max. But Desmonte, he is someone who values her, understands her and appreciates her for who she is. These years that came along were fulfilling together, but had a few bumps along the road. Desmonte had lower back issues from years ago that got worse over time because he didn't really help it recover. He moved several times by himself, picking up heavy loads without being cautious of his spine. Medical research and statistics showed that 70%, or maybe higher now, of the population in this world have a herniation in their backs, but it sometimes goes unnoticed if not exacerbated. Desmonte had to go through minimally-invasive surgery to help his back get better and reduce the herniation. This would be the second time getting back surgery, but this time it would be better because Desmarie is by his side to help him with anything. The recovery went more than well; as a super hero himself why wouldn't it?

Not long after, Desmarie did her US citizenship with the help of Victor. Yes, they both kept in touch. After all, he was her step-father and he did put a roof over her head for a long time after her mom's tragic death. And most important, he loved Desmarie and her mom so much and helped both of them as much as he possibly could until he couldn't any more. But with Maria at least, it was too late unfortunately. Victor was the last closest thing Desmarie still had to her mom. She still loved him of course, and him the same to her. Desmarie chose never to ask him in all honesty why he let his family member kick her out. That's it, it was water under the bridge, and Desmarie is more than fine to where she is now in life; thankful actually. He would actually visit Florida as he used to for the winters, even additional times during the year since he had some family living down here. Victor ended up meeting Desmonte and liked him right away, "A real gentleman" he would always say. Desmarie loves it. Victor and her would meet up occasionally for lunch and talk. He would also be there to help and get in contact with if she had any questions about repairing anything in the apartment; even financial help for the bigger stuff if needed. But Desmarie chose to limit herself with that, she didn't want any additional problems with the part of his family that didn't like her. Victor still however stuck around and always helped Desmarie, even in the end she would never forget about that.

Desmarie got another job, after being in the hospital for almost 4 years. She accepted an offer at a call center for a big insurance company. It was her first call center job, and it was pretty decent, except the fact that a lot of times she would get inbound calls from idiotic individuals who just didn't have anything else to do throughout their day. But anyway, she was there for almost 2 years and ended up becoming a trainer for new hires at the end. That was fun, only having to take 10-15 calls for the day, with the remainder of the day just making friends and having fun, while also helping them ease in to their job objectives at the office.

One of the mornings during her drive to work, Desmarie passed by the big building next to the call center office with a bulletin glimmering outside showing "PTA program starting September 2014." Desmarie thought for a moment as to what that was. Rehabilitation, physical therapy, yeah, she remembers. She recalls going a few times with Lilly when she repeatedly messed up her ankle. That was pretty cool and chill, the therapists would be there to help and assist someone into functional recovery. There wasn't any traumatic emergencies nor blood or stress like in hospitals with doctors and nurses. This was part of the healthcare field, Desmarie reassured herself that the idea sounded really good to her. She went in to apply, got forms from a staff member to fill out and turn in, then exited the door and drove to work which was the building right next to the university.

After form completions, taking two entrance exams and interviewing with the program director, Desmarie got into the PTA program! It wasn't easy, since she was part of the first Cohort to certify the school for the national board exams and grant course completion. This was something new, but from that morning where Desmarie first saw the bulletin and applied, she wanted it. This would be a great career choice for her, it has everything she likes. Plus, she would learn and become a clinical expert, literally, in rehab exercises that would aide and help her boyfriend Desmonte. So hopefully there wouldn't be any lower back issues arising, god willing. She would learn the importance of body mechanic usage and recovery techniques for any orthopedic and neurological deficit of a patient. Physical therapy would focus on getting back the functional mobility of a patient that has had an acute injury and/or wants to recover from chronic issues, as well as lessening pain levels with modality usage.

The program was super stressful but so interesting and fun that Desmarie loved it. Beyond it being incredibly tough, everything had to be done and completed by the books since Desmarie's class was in charge of getting the university certified for the PTA program as she was part of the first class ever to start learning for that program. There were multiple, sorry, hundreds of nights spent with tears drowning Desmarie's weak and tired eyes while studying in front of her notes and large textbooks. Desmarie was on her way to almost finishing, but the light at the end of the tunnel couldn't be further away. It felt like forever and the exams never seemed to end. A big part of that planning was that this course that was selected by Desmarie was accelerated, and the entire class would finish in just 2 years. Having God bless her daily and always after that, Desmarie did not give up. She can share with everyone all one thing, one important thing she had while attending a stressful program during college years. That was Desmonte; her love and support. Having someone stand by you at home and anywhere else is so important to have while trying to accomplish something big. Without that, honestly, it just ends up not being successful. If you do make it, it doesn't last for long in her opinion. Lack of faith and energy into it, will end up draining it until it ends.

The holiday season was upon them, and Desmarie was attending the second year of the program. It was right before getting into the bigger and much harder classes. After Halloween and Thanksgiving holidays passed, something ended up happening big during Christmas time.

CHAPTER 23

The Question

Christmas Eve that year, early Christmas morning passed 1:00am, Desmonte and Desmarie spent hours with his family eating and drinking. After celebrating the holiday season, they went home. Desmonte and Desmarie stepped into the living room and began opening the gifts from under their tree. Gifts inside the stocking were always the first to open just because; it was a save the best for last kind of thing. When it came down to it, Desmarie became a very generous person with him; especially with gift-giving. Giving to Desmonte is never too much, just like those complicated high school mathematical functions, the limit does not exist. Desmarie is also a very competitive person, meaning with any video game, board game, challenges and even giving gifts, she likes to win it. Out of so much love, both Desmarie and Desmonte have a similar characteristic with each other, and both of them loved spoiling the other to the maximum level.

Desmarie goes to reach for her stocking hanging on the wall, which had one gift waiting for her. She starts to feel a small box inside. She catches hold of this precious little blessing, looks at it and gasps. "Oh my god, really?!" Desmarie is startled as she looks at what she is holding in front of her. It was a small glistening grey box, printed "Zales" in the exterior front. Water begins to form in Desmarie's eyes as she opens the box. Staring right at her was a beautiful white gold ring with a diamond in the middle, surrounded by sapphire stones. She turns to look up at Desmonte smiling so wide, his grin took up his entire angelic face. "Will you marry me?" Desmonte asked with his voice sounding nervous and excited at the same time. He happily waits for her response, but he didn't have to wait long. This moment felt so amazing and fulfilling. Desmarie could not have been happier; she has continued to cherish the many blessings that have come her way. She wants nothing more than to be happy with Desmonte, and also try to make him as happy as he makes her; if that is even remotely possible. The warm embrace surrounded the room, and all Desmarie can see was Desmonte. "Yes, of course yes!" Desmarie stands in shock as Desmonte takes her left hand and puts the ring on her finger. "Is this really happening?" Desmarie asks while her voice begins to crackle. She tries to get herself together at least for the video being taken by Desmonte's phone in the background. "Yes, it's happening because I love you so much and you mean the world to me," Desmonte states to her with gleefulness overfilling his deep tone of voice. Desmarie goes to hug Desmonte, wrapping her arms around his neck and plants a soft long but deep kiss on his lips. She has never felt so good. "Some people wait a lifetime, for a moment like this" (Kelly Clarkson, 2002). Being in Desmonte's arms brings butterflies to her stomach. The butterfly, such a beautiful and meaningful symbol in this lifetime. It shows up during happy times, but it also shows up during hard times. No matter the moment, the butterfly always pushed Desmarie to happiness. Maria is always there, forever guiding her.

"Good judgement comes from experience, and a lot of that comes from bad judgement," a quote from Will Rogers. With bad, comes a lot of good, and that is something that Desmarie has believed fully because of course it all has happened to her. Desmonte has taken her breath away. From the beginning when he accepted her, the baggage behind her and everything else. This true love has given both Desmonte and Desmarie a clear view of what love is supposed to be like.

CHAPTER 24

Back Together Again

The year 2016 held an amazing celebration but also had a sad loss. The end of May carried out Desmarie's college graduation, however, the official ceremony was happening in June. She felt so accomplished, it was indeed a stressful year in the program at the university. But with the help and support from Desmonte, she was able to conquer it all much easier and get to where she wanted to be at the end. Countless nights were spent studying in the bedroom, lights in low dim while wearing her pretty Bose headphones playing relaxing acoustic music along with white noise in the background. That was the only way for Desmarie to study the never-ending material of rehabilitation topics. The board exam came a little less than a month right after graduation. On July 6, 2016, Desmarie was scheduled to go in and take it at 8:00-8:30am; that was the time she voluntarily chose. It was 4 hours long with 200 questions of material learned in a matter of two years. It has been truly incredible where the road has taken her to. It was finally here; this is what she wanted to become. This determines her life-long career if she can have it or would she have to let it go? There was no putting a stop to Desmarie as she drove to the testing site that morning. At a red light, Desmarie looks over to her right at a grass patch and sees a white butterfly. She smiled, placed her hand on her chest to feel her heart beat; beating faster as the light turned green.

Arriving at the building, Desmarie lets Desmonte know that she got there ok, then turns off her phone to put it in the locker along with her other belongings. The test begins at 8 on the dot, Desmarie remains calm as she is fully aware that all of the material needed to learn and know for this test was already in her brain. A professor told her during the 2 years, if you don't know the answer to a complex question, stop for a moment, breathe and think. The answer is there somewhere inside your subconscious, dig it up and find it wherever it is. Desmarie remained confident in those hours; she had to. A 15-minute lunch break came along, but Desmarie didn't take it. Instead, she stood up to stretch in front of her computer and took several deep breaths for a few minutes closing her eyes, then sat down on her seat to continue the board exam. Finishing a little bit before the time was up, Desmarie gets up from her seat feeling good. It was a pretty tough test, but nothing that she couldn't handle. It was challenging but good to take and to know the information given. Thinking to herself, "I've done and studied too much to get where I am now and not making it, I got this, I definitely got this," Desmarie did not think twice about this. Passing the boards was never a "what if" scenario, Desmarie did not accept anything less than passing it. She believed in herself from the beginning, and having the support from her loving family members aided in remaining optimistic. Before exiting the building, she went to get her belongings from the locker and checked out with a staff member. She was advised that the results would be listed on the website account and emailed to her in 3 weeks.

Finally, July 28th came along, 3 weeks after taking the board exam. The day couldn't have come any sooner. It was also Maria's anniversary of death. The day of tragic loss to Desmarie took place 14 years ago; she couldn't believe so many years have passed by. Some days it feels like it was just yesterday. Other days it felt like it happened a lifetime ago. As each year passes, and this terrible anniversary arrived annually to Desmarie and others, it hits her hard. This date was always sad and dark; depressing and painful to the gut. "Being a candle is not easy: In order to give light, one must first burn" (Rumi, 13th Century). Poetry is beautiful, and when the words can be relatable, it's even more beautiful to the soul. July 28th now would no longer be a sad and dark day; nope.

It will now be a day with a creeping small ray of sunshine trying to take over a large field of grass. Desmarie and Desmonte at that time were walking back home from exercising around the lake nearby where they lived. Desmarie's phone goes off and an email alert sounds. It was an email from the testing sight. In green, bold and capital lettering, a 6-letter word appears on the screen when Desmarie scrolled down in the page: "PASSED". Desmarie stops short from walking and puts her phone down. Tears begin to spill out from her light hazel eyes, a delicious taste when they slid towards her mouth. She lets out a gasp of happiness while looking up at the sky. Clouds crowded over, blocking the sun at the moment. "Yes! thank you God, thank you mom, thank you, thank you!" she goes to hug Desmonte who was standing right next to her. Desmonte smiles and embraces her touch. "Of course, you passed, because you are amazing baby!" Desmonte declares as he kisses her lips. A sweet shiver runs down her spine as tears continue to run down her cheeks.

Yes, the feeling was bitter sweet. It felt great graduating, and then finding out that she passed her Boards. The same week, Desmarie had to sign up to take the Florida State Exam for her career to learn all of the laws in the practice. After taking it, Desmarie receives an email a week later stating that she passed. In comparison to the boards, the state exam was a piece of cake, just a bit boring overall. She obtained her medical license and was ready to look for her next job with a larger opportunity at hand. Unfortunately, in those same weeks, she received some bad news. Victor wasn't doing so well; it happened suddenly at the beginning of that year. He was going to attend Desmarie's college graduation but regrettably, his family refused to take him out to that event since he still felt ill and weak. Luckily, Desmarie spoke with Victor and also went to visit him several times that same year. He started feeling sick the year prior, but would end up recovering and come to remission to whatever was carrying him down. But when this year hit them, the illness didn't seem to go away; his age as well wasn't hiding anymore. His medical condition plateaued according to doctors. He developed pneumonia regularly and had digestive issues as well. Given his old age, the doctors didn't know what else to do but thought to just keep him comfortable for the time being since all other medicines and injections weren't really helping him. Desmarie was put into an emotionally state of stress, where she wanted to visit Victor at the hospital. She knew it would be distressing and agonizing for her to step foot into a hospital to see a family member feeling helpless; she knew memories would come back and she didn't want that, not now. But this was her step-father, this was mom's husband, a man that she fell in love with. Victor was the last thing she had closest to her mom. Why is this time coming so fast, too fast? At home, Desmonte encouraged Desmarie to visit him and nudged her lightly to go to the hospital, just in case. Desmonte knew that if something were to happen let's say overnight or sometime this week and she never got to go and see him for the final and last time, Desmarie would truly regret it. Thank you Desmonte, for always being so good and so thoughtful to her. Thank goodness that he exists in her life, Desmarie ended up taking his advice and went to visit him about a week or two before he passed away.

Desmarie walked into the hospital, got her visitor sticker and went to Victor's room upstairs. She goes to open his door and there he was, lying down with his eyes closed. Probably sleeping, but maybe awake but just doesn't have the energy to be fully conscious and alert. Desmarie knows that he can hear his surroundings, no matter in what state. The heavy noise of supplemental oxygen and machines echoed in the background surrounding them both. Desmarie begins to speak in a soft tone of voice, quiet so nobody outside in the halls can hear. "Hi Victor, it's me, I am so sorry you are like this right now, I love you so much. I want to thank you for the last time for everything you've done for me, for mom, for all of us. You are good and we all love you. Thank you, please just relax and know that I am here and I love you." Desmarie holds his hand while continuing to express her emotions to him. She stays there for some more time and continues talking to him. It starts to eventually get difficult for her, she tries to control her feelings from splurging out and she goes ahead to wipe the tears from her face away quickly. Desmarie kisses his forehead and says goodbye to Victor. A week or two passes, Desmarie and Desmonte attended her nephew's birthday party at a park. While walking by the little beach area, she takes her phone out to see a text message from Victor's oldest daughter, letting her know that Victor had passed away. Desmarie drops to her knees with both her hands holding her face tight. A person should cry it all out, if they don't, it just simply isn't healthy. It will bombard you some other day and disturb your sleep. Desmarie begins to sob quietly then loudly, she couldn't believe that Victor was gone. Desmonte and Desmarie's sisters stay close by and comfort her. "Well, that's it then. I know now that they are finally together again," Desmarie had remarked while rubbing her eyes. Her sister Babi smiled, listening to what Desmarie just said. She knew that mom was so happy with him. Victor has finally reunited with Maria in paradise now. Desmarie clenched her fists and hits the ground, staying quiet for a bit. "Thank you, baby, for convincing me to go there and see him," Desmarie mentions to Desmonte as she mourns her step-father. Desmonte nods as he placed both his arms around Desmarie and hugs her tight with no signs of letting go. "Of course, my love," continuing to reassure her while planting a long kiss on Desmarie's head.

CHAPTER 25

Traveling is Leaving Any Worries Behind

Desmarie now has been working at her first health clinic as an official clinician. She accepted a great offer while still working at another hospital after leaving the call center job since she had to attend school full-time. It felt amazing to leave her final "normal" and typical office job and dive into her career; start showing the world what she learned and what she loves to do. Desmarie perceived this feeling like a famous athlete who was crossing the finish line in a marathon; success. Desmonte also got a better job that were no longer accepting ridiculous 12-hour work shifts as well. In life, you have to know and expect that you will be starting from down, and work your way up to better opportunities. A person can't expect to have a house and become rich right away when you start out in life; of course, exempting oneself from growing up from a rich parent. At the end of the day, you will only be looked at as a receiver of inheritance from the hard work spilt from your parents. Legacy and title given to you is not a true accomplishment. Little by little in the real world, hard work does pay off.

Coming up close to ending the year 2016, although sad moments happened, exciting ones took place for recovery afterwards. Desmonte and Desmarie saved up for a major vacation that was very much needed for the end of the year. They both took a trip to NYC with Desmarie's sister Patty and her family. It was the month of November, and Desmarie began to reminisce when she used to live in New Jersey. During these months, the weather became chilly and temperatures would dip around in the 30's at night, 40's during the day; also depending where you were in the state. In the city, it was always windy and you end up always being on the move. It was a beautiful trip and everyone enjoyed themselves very much. NYC is always so great to see and be in; the presence of itself is just like no other.

Desmonte and Desmarie also planned a surprise visit to her family in New Jersey for their last night stay before traveling back home to Miami. Once they saw each other, Desmarie jumped into Ruth's warm hug and stayed in it. Desmarie missed them so much, seeing them again felt like just yesterday when she was living there again and seeing them daily. She and Desmonte promised them that they would see them sooner than later since their wedding was going to be planned this upcoming year. Having ideas already in mind, the couple discussed it with them to see what would work best at the end.

After leaving New Jersey, Desmonte and Desmarie then took a trip to Disney World the week after. They both went park hopping to all 4 parks and stayed at a Disney resort for 4 days. Waking up at 7am never felt so easy to do. There is a social media posted out there that jokes around and says: a person puts 5-10 different alarms to wake up for work, but when they are at Disney World, only one alarm is needed to get up. Disney World is Desmarie's happy place, and she was beyond blessed to have someone by her side who also was a big little kid at heart and loved the Disney parks as well.

Arriving back to reality and starting work again, Desmarie felt tired. It felt like such a long work week back after taking two big vacations. Although rested, you just fully don't have enough vacationing in your life. One day during a work week, Desmarie gets a text alert from Desmonte. Before unlocking her phone and opening the link that was sent from him at that moment, she reads the link and notices the word "travel" in it. When she pressed on the hyperlink, her jaw immediately drops. It was a flight and hotel itinerary…. for Europe! Whoa no way! Italy! This was Desmarie's dream. She had always told Desmonte that when she was younger, her dream and part of her bucket list was to visit Rome in Italy, sit down at a restaurant outside and eat homemade pasta while over-looking the Colosseum. Was this really happening? Desmarie lost sight as to where she was at the moment, and felt like she was immediately lifted up in to the air in complete daydream mode. "Ahh oh my god I can't wait to pack!" Desmarie yells out, her words echoed throughout the clinic and her patients look up and congratulate her.

CHAPTER 26

Vero Amore Sotto le Stelle, Che Bella Notte

Getting to the security gate, Desmarie and Desmonte begin to loosen their laces from their shoes as they approach the airport security checkpoint before their terminal. Having already checked their big suitcases, Desmarie places her small carry on onto the conveyor while Desmonte places his shoes and phone onto the basket to be scanned. Being right on time, they both walk up to the terminal in the international region of the airport, and sit down to wait. "Colosseum here we come!" Desmonte says aloud unable to contain his excitement. Desmarie was in lala land as she was updating her Facebook status excitedly. As the main flight attendant announced their row of seats, Desmonte and Desmarie both stand up and walk up to the ticket stand. Desmarie looks out to the window where the planes are getting ready to take off, then turns to peer at the passenger boarding bridge.

Desmonte puts away both itineraries safe into his pocket and holds hands with Desmarie. They look at each other and smile wide; people looking were able to count how many teeth they had inside their mouths. Looking and observing this couple, that is Desmonte and Desmarie, it sends out a sweet reminder to the world around them that true love is out there for anyone and everyone. Both of them look so in love, it's absolutely incomparable to anything else that is great. Desmonte gives Desmarie a kiss on her forehead and takes her hair to put behind her ears. As they both find their seats, they finally relax and plan out what they're going to be doing in the 9 days that they will be in Italy. Desmarie before leaving their place, made a very well-organized agenda planner of what their destinations were going to be while in Rome and other cities. The plans were for day 1 to get settled into their hotel room. Afterwards, go and visit the Colosseum, Vatican City, Florence, and Pisa. During all of those trips and destinations in between, they would obviously be enjoying the historic landmarks which included St. Peter's Basilica, the Pantheon, Piazza Navona, the Roman Forum, and of course the world-class art inside and outside of the buildings, in addition to the ruins of the Colosseum. The flight in TAP Portugal airlines included a connecting flight from Lisbon, Portugal to get to Rome, Italy. Arriving at the airport in the capital of Portugal, Desmarie and Desmonte went to get something to eat, as well as window shopped a bit throughout the stores close to the terminal for the hour being there.

Both of them finally arrived at their hotel in Rome by taxi, coming from the airport. Villa San Lorenzo Maria Hotel was such a cozy and super nice place they stayed in. Being located from a small bus ride away from the Colosseum, this hotel was in its own little area in the outskirts of the city. Desmonte purchased a ticket to ride the trollies throughout the metropolis to get to familiar destinations close by, and Uber to go anywhere else that was further away; especially late at night to be safe. What they didn't take to account was that all the cities in Europe were a ways away. When people that vacation look at a map of Europe, almost none of them come to realize that every place has quite a bit of distance in between them; at least the tourist attractions. But this didn't stop them nor did it create any interruption for their itinerary. Luckily, Uber was available in Italy at that time so the couple saved a good amount of money while being there; avoiding high priced taxis.

The Colosseum was absolutely breath-taking. Walking across the sidewalk and crossing the street, Desmonte and Desmarie found a small restaurant close by that sat both indoor and outdoor; right in front of the Colosseum. They stopped and asked a waiter for seats and a menu. The brisk cool wind blew by and pulled Desmarie's hair onto the front of her face. Desmonte giggles as he takes her hair away from her face. "Are you cold? Let's go get a sweater, I think I saw some stores nearby," Desmonte looks ahead and sees small shops next to the restaurant. "Don't worry, let's eat first then we can go, I am actually good with this long sleeve. Plus, drinking wine will help," Desmarie commented as she plants a big kiss on his lips. They both sit down and order their meals. The couple ended up both ordering a pasta carbonara. While sipping her wine, Desmarie looks up to her left side and glances at the beautiful and historic Colosseum. Such a beautiful sight! For a building that dates back more than 2,000 years ago, the Colosseum was a dream to finally go see in person. Desmonte and Desmarie have never seen such ancient beauty. "Thank you baby for this. I feel like a million thank you's isn't going to be enough to express my gratitude for this trip," Desmarie's eyes get watery but then gets halted by Desmonte's warm hands. Her heart skips a beat while turning back to look at Desmonte smiling. Dreams do come true. Desmonte takes a selfie of the two of them with the Colosseum in the background, and with the remaining battery life left in her phone, Desmarie posts it immediately on her social media page.

Being in Italy means being able to see and discover Renaissance art. It was truly a flourishing and blooming period of time from the past; the 15th and 16th centuries were prodigious yet unbelievable. The skill and talent of the legendary masters that we know as Michelangelo and Raphael were truly amazing artisans. If only they were still around to meet and get a picture taken with, or even an aesthetic autograph from them. As the couple toured the Vatican, its own city state as explained by their tour guide, Desmonte and Desmarie began to discover and explore the beautiful craftsmanship of statues surrounding the outside of the building as well as the inside; while being enveloped by the beauty of paintings covering the walls and ceilings of the building. Finally, their tour guide instructor leads them to the steps going into the Sistine Chapel. Unable to take photos nor videos due to copyright laws inside, it didn't bother them. Both Desmonte and Desmarie stared in astonishment as they locked eyes with the view of The Last Judgement image. Incredible, extraordinary art by Michelangelo; although the story about him creating it wasn't so pleasant as he was forced for days and months on end to finish it. Desmarie considers him to be one of the most special and talented humans that lived on this Earth. In life, you might not be able to get done what you want to get done. Or, you won't be able to become what you want to become or show off what you always wanted to show off. But what is important to notice is how the ride was, the experience of it all. How you lived the rest of your life and the journey to and from many other different destinations, and the skillsets that you gained throughout the process. "Life is not measured by the number of breaths we take, but by the moments that take our breath away," a quote by the poet Maya Angelou.

Continuing their amazing trip in Italy, Desmonte and Desmarie climbed 320 steps onto the very top of St. Peter's Basilica Dome. What was so funny about this was at first, the couple read at the entrance that there were 551 steps to complete. But there were two options for climbing the Dome, you either choose to climb all the steps, or take an elevator. Little did they know, the elevator only went up to the first floor. After that, 320 steps were left to climb up. Dripping sweat and breathing heavily, Desmonte and Desmarie finally get to the top. With so much laughter along the way, they managed to climb the steps and also began to wonder if they should consider moving here so they can complete this cardio exercise weekly to lose weight. Giggling non-stop together, they take a moment and look down from the dome of Saint Peter's Basilica at the giant view. Seeing Saint Peter's Square with the Vatican Obelisk at the center, they can't believe their eyes. What an incredible sight! And well worth climbing 320 steps for.

Desmarie couldn't stop thinking of what great timing that Desmonte had chosen to travel to Italy during the year. Being here in the month of March was amazing. The sky was a clear blue painting all day, and temperatures dropped to the 40's in the evenings; which was perfect weather for both of them since they were used to the chilly weather temperatures from up north. Strolling through the cobblestone streets and alley ways, Desmonte and Desmarie shopped a bit through some stores but then came across to an outdoor location where there were huge crowds of tourists taking pictures. Curious to find out where they actually were at the moment since they weren't sure, Desmarie went to her map's app in her smart phone and walked towards the location in front of them. The sound of splashing waters emerged upon their ears as they got closer. Wow, what a beautiful and big fountain. As Desmarie goes to her search engine and types what they have come across, she couldn't believe what she read. They both just ended up next to the famous Trevi Fountain! "Wow this is so spectacular!" Desmonte overwhelmed with how mesmerizing the beauty of the fountain had, with its incredible architecture and story behind it. Desmonte gathered some change from his pockets for both of them to toss to the fountain right after making a wish.

The couple took a bus to the port of Napoli the next day. Even the bus ride was great, they both were able to see amazing landmarks from afar. One of them being the famous but terrifying volcano of Vesuvius, which erupted a long time ago in history that caused the ancient Roman city of Pompeii to be buried under a thick carpet of volcanic ash. Viewing it from miles away was kind of scary but also exciting. Finally arriving to the port, Desmonte and Desmarie get off the bus and stretch after the hour and a half bus ride, which wasn't bad at all considering it was still morning and the seats felt like a coach bus; super comfortable. Looking forward to traveling down south of the Gulf of Naples onto the island of Capri, Desmarie got her phone ready for pictures as Desmonte was organizing their planner and also purchasing the tickets for the boat ride to the island. A nice, warm breeze blew through as the couple got off the boat and onto the island where they awaited the tour guide to begin. The island of Capri was absolutely stunning. It reminded Desmarie of the Caribbean islands, so many hills overlooking the crystal-clear blue waters of the ocean. The couple also got to eat and enjoy a big delicious Italian cuisine during the mid-day when stopping for a late lunch break into a restaurant going halfway downhill. Also, not going to forget to mention, the famous Limoncello drink originated from this island here. Such a delicious natural liqueur, drinking it felt so soothing trickling down the throat but yet so intense with the tartness of the lemons mixed in. Anything citrus-flavored could do no wrong for Desmonte since he was a big fanatic. He enjoys all that is sweet and fruity.

Following the island visit the couple took during the week, they made a stop to Florence, Italy to see some famous statues. They also wanted to try the pizza from there as well. Desmonte and Desmarie got to the city by bullet train. The way that the transportation ran here was so easy and convenient; super quick to get from city to city, thank goodness. In the city of Florence, the lovely pair made several stops to visit the cathedrals while exploring the amazing art. Each building that they stepped foot in, was covered in amazing painted art from the ceilings to the walls surrounding the visitors. David of Michelangelo was located in that same city, which was listed in their planner to go and visit. That statue stood out and made every other sculpture around it oblivious; he caught everyone's attention right away. The biblical figure was hypnotizing to look at, with his captivating body figure built of marble, Michelangelo once again satisfies the audience with his amazing talent. This was the city where Desmonte and Desmarie sat down and ate a slice of pizza each. My lord, the pizza here was exquisite! Desmarie thought she had tasted the best pizza when she visited Staten Island with her family. But no, she stood corrected. The pizza here did not compare to anywhere else; not even New York. Desmonte and Desmarie later that afternoon visited some old towns by Tuscany where they went inside some museums and temples, looking at more sculptures portraying famous figures from history. An incredible sight to see was observing the Discobolus. Desmarie was blown away when seeing the statue. The mold and carve to show all of the human muscles stood out and the accuracy of the anatomy amazed her. Being a clinician herself and having to learn and memorize over 520 muscles of the human body including where they all are, she found it mind-blowing that people from centuries ago where able to craft these statues and get every muscle detail perfectly on the body.

More days passed and Desmonte was loving this trip himself more and more. He couldn't be happier spending this amazing time with

Desmarie in such a beautiful and romantic place. The graceful twosome explored the Pantheon one of their afternoons, then afterwards met up with some old friend's from Desmarie that she met through her sister Babi while the sisters were living together in St. Thomas. They are an old couple that originally lived in Rome, but would visit the Caribbean islands annually for their yearly vacation. Super kind and generous individuals, they met up with Desmonte and Desmarie to have dinner at a restaurant nearby. The menu and courses included gnocchi with cheese and ravioli with red sauce. The friends around the table also ordered a big bottle of wine, along with some other cold cuts for appetizers. Everyone's plate was wiped clean before the night was over. Two bottles of wine were gone within an hour or so while the couple spoke about their wonderful trip so far. Waiters came by to continue serving them and making sure their glasses were full at the right amount with wine. Entering the restaurant, you were able to hear both couples laughing and speaking both Italian and Spanish to each other. Laughter and sounds of wine glasses clinking together to cheer this wonderful time and moment spent with great friends, love, and good food.

The last days remaining of their vacation, Desmarie and Desmonte made a stop to visit the Roman Forum which was located next to the Colosseum. It was a stunning sight to see, with columns from buildings still somewhat standing upright; what was left of them at least. Desmarie admired so much seeing history left untouched and imperfect at the same time. She closed her eyes slowly and imagined what was once ancient Rome, what was once a giant Roman Empire in the B.C. era with emperors ruling their kingdoms. That was always Desmarie's favorite subject to learn about in middle school during her 7th grade social studies class. Desmonte then guided Desmarie up several steps made of stone onto a beautiful small garden outside, over-looking the entire Roman Forum. Desmarie placed both of her arms around Desmonte and kissed him. What a beautiful day it was, and since their European vacation was coming close to an end, Desmarie couldn't help but feel sort of sad in that moment. Being with Desmonte though, it always patches up anything negative felt around her. Desmarie handed her phone to a tourist couple walking by to ask them to take a picture of them. This happens periodically as Desmarie got this funny but sometimes annoying habit from her sister Babi who always does this everywhere she goes. It was ok though, taking photos was fun and a great way to capture memories. The best part about that is being able to go back and look into it and re-live it in the future.

As Desmonte and Desmarie got back to the hotel, they emptied their bags and began to organize their baggage with souvenirs a little. Not looking forward to it, Desmarie laid down on the bed and started watching the Spartacus show on T.V. Desmonte joined her while taking off his shoes. All of a sudden, one of their stomachs growls as it echoes throughout the room. Desmarie giggles and asks Desmonte, "Do you want to go to the supermarket next door here and get some snacks to bring back to the room?" Desmonte gets up from the bed and goes to where his shoes are, "Definitely, we still have some money left," smirking at his hand as it leaves his pocket. Both of them head out of the hotel and onto the sidewalk right outside the gate. The stars in the sky were sparkling and bright that night. The dark azure above the lovely city at night sent both of them off with a cool evening breeze. Walking inside the supermarket, Desmarie grabs a bottle of olive oil to take home with them, as well as a bottle of wine for her sister Babi as a thanks for taking care of their furry little family member. In the front of the cashier, Desmonte places a bottle of wine picked out for tonight, some prosciutto and cheese too to go with it.

There was true love under the stars, what a beautiful night. Inside the hotel room, the lights were turned off, but the TV played in the background with Spartacus still showing. Eating and drinking, Desmonte and Desmarie shared their love in every way possible and imaginably speaking. His touch sent Desmarie over the moon as Desmarie slowly and carefully puts her wine glass down. She then gets close to his face and teases him. Desmarie's kiss gave Desmonte the warm and loving touch he craved for years before meeting her. In between finishing up the food and the entire bottle of wine, they were no longer watching the TV in the background. Desmonte's hands traced onto Desmarie's skin as their lips continued to interlock. She sunk her face into his tender touch. The night was full of love, almost forgetting the fact that they had to catch a plane in the early afternoon the next day.

CHAPTER 27

What Happens in Rome, Goes Back with You

Flying back home to Miami, the trip inside the plane was delightedly comfortable thankfully. Unfortunately, Desmarie felt some discomfort in her lower abdomen since it was getting to be the time of the month for her soon. Sleeping for most of the trip back to the states, Desmonte joined her to nap while holding hands. The movie Rio played in the background in the airline's screen on their seats. At about 7 and a half hours later, the couple arrived to Miami.

A month passes by and the weather begins to warm up tremendously in Florida. Desmonte and Desmarie had organized their souvenirs, placing them where they felt they looked their best inside their apartment. They also saved photos from their Italy trip, putting some in frames, but all the others on their desktop computer. It was almost the end of the month of April and Desmarie continued feeling some menstrual pains throughout that week. It felt odd because she would usually get a pain maybe once in the week right before getting her thing. She had noticed she was a week and a half late; her cycle would always be like that; sometimes even being 2 weeks once or twice in her life. But this time was different. Even though it was only a week and half late, she felt more frequent pains in her lower abdomen. Not being able to recall feeling like this times before, she went to the store to buy a pregnancy test; just in case. That Wednesday night, both Desmonte and Desmarie watched a movie, then went to bed to wake up early the next morning for work. It was a Thursday, luckily getting close to Friday and the weekend to rest. Desmarie presses off on her morning alarm and goes to the bathroom right away to pee on the stick. Waiting outside, she put on her underwear and socks while slipping into her polo work shirt. Desmarie then walks back into the bathroom and gets the stick from the tub. The stick shows: "Yes+." Desmarie lets out a small quiet gasp, surprised but also seen smiling. "Oh my god, this is crazy!" Desmarie while smirking runs to the bed to gently wake Desmonte up. "Baby, I took a test, I am pregnant," Desmarie whispers slowly but anxiously to not startle him in the moment. Desmonte's cheeks get wrinkly and widen as his smile makes the sunrise outside even more beautiful than what it actually was. "What? Oh my god really?! That's great!" Desmonte's excited and comforting tone of voice lessened Desmarie's worried look on her face. "What's wrong baby? This is good, we are going to have a baby!" Desmarie smiles and nods in agreement. "I am just surprised; being with you though makes this so amazing and feel so right. This is good right?" Desmarie asks him nervously. "Of course, this is good, you are so amazing to me. We are going to be parents!" Desmonte pulls Desmarie into the bed and under the sheets to cuddle. When moments like this happen in life, anyone can tell you that every woman on this earth should have and be with a man like Desmonte. Someone who gives such a calming presence and unconditional love to his girl. Desmarie felt beyond blessed to be with him, to experience this with him. This was a good thing, but catching Desmarie off guard, she couldn't help but feel shocked and surprised in the beginning. She doesn't want to be with any other partner in her life, she wants to be with Desmonte. Both of them hugged tight and burrowed next to each other before Desmarie had to finally leave for work.

Desmarie went to her boss's office and spoke to her about the news. Admiringly, it was easy and Desmarie ended up having her full support, in addition from everyone else she worked with at the clinic. Desmarie had scheduled an appointment to see her new gynecologist on May

1st. Her oldest sister Patty recommended her OB doctor to Desmarie since, shocker, Patty was also pregnant! She was having her third child while Desmarie was having her first. Patty got pregnant a month before it happened to Desmarie. It is so crazy how everything comes to play in the world. Knowing this road ahead could be bumpy and tough, Desmarie was blessed to share her pregnancy with her own sister, as well as having her soon-to-be fiancé Desmonte by her side. Her oldest sister was a great guide and help during the pregnancy. She also helped Desmarie to check if everything that was being felt was ok. When Desmarie contacted her family in New Jersey to give them the exciting new news, they all celebrated happily over the phone. Ruth and Lilly wished all of their love and congratulations to the lovely couple. She also made sure to promise that they would be there for their wedding in the coming months, also to visit them the following year to meet the beautiful new member of the family. Desmarie's due date was December 24th, 2017.

During Desmarie's first appointment to the OB specialist, she immediately felt super comfortable with him and his nursing staff. The main nurse who attended to Desmarie regularly actually had Maria's middle name, which Desmarie thought was a crazy coincidence. It was a clear sign that she was with the right doctor and nurses to take on together on this amazing pregnancy journey. The nurse provided a cup for Desmarie to complete a urine test to confirm the positive result that came out a week ago at home. Minutes after Desmarie handed her sample to the nurse, she went back to her exam room to sit down and wait. "Congratulations, you are going to be a mommy!" the heavy Spanish accent is gentle and comforting to hear as the nurse walks into the exam room. She was holding up a bag full of goodies inside, which included some brochures and info about pregnancy, as well as a discount card and pre-natal vitamins to take for the next nine months and maybe after. Desmarie was grateful beyond belief. She gratefully took the gift bag and thanked the nurse.

Two days later, Desmarie went to get a transvaginal ultrasound at the OB office with Desmonte accompanying her. The procedure didn't feel pleasant, but Desmarie was willing to be distracted with something else like Desmonte talking to her. The staff in that hospital also made their patients feel good and relaxed, they always stayed kind and professional at the same time. The ultrasound technician clicks on her monitor and shows the couple the small embryo presenting itself on the screen. She points to it and confirms, "And that is your baby!" Both Desmarie and Desmonte awe in surprise as they smile big at the black and white live video on the screen. Heartbeat sounds comes out of the speakers and Desmarie looks at Desmonte with her eyes big and wide. Life is so incredible and precious. They both had no clue that a 6-week-old embryo had a heartbeat already. Desmonte goes to kiss Desmarie's forehead as the tech takes pictures from the live video to print out and hand to the couple.

CHAPTER 28

Eternal Bond

During the 9-month journey, Desmarie enjoyed being pregnant. Not only did she get to have a cute baby bump, but she also received special treatment out in the stores; such as the supermarket where almost everyone let her cut them in line for the cashier to check out. And when home, tender loving care 24/7.

The month of June had arrived, and it was going to be one of most special months of both Desmarie and Desmonte's life ever. They were finally going to get married! Proposed to almost 2 years prior, Desmarie couldn't wait to finally marry the man of her dreams. Desmonte would disagree and let the audience know that he was more excited. The wedding was getting planned right before making the trips of NY, Disney and Europe. It was going to take place 2017 this year sometime in the spring and/or summer. When the big news came out, the date was set to get married in June. To save money since they were going to be having a baby, Desmonte and Desmarie were going to make it official in the County Clerk's Office in south Miami. They invited close family which included Desmarie's from New Jersey to come and be here for the special event. The reception afterwards would be a bigger deal. Lilly was so happy to see Desmarie and Desmonte after not seeing her sister for about a year or so. The family had bought Desmarie a dress to wear for the ceremony. Amazingly, it ended up being a perfect fit with a 3-month pregnant belly to worry about. The magical day finally came. Desmarie had slept over with her family at the Hilton close by, of course it was mandatory to sleep away from the soon-to-be husband the night before the wedding. Lilly did Desmarie's hair beautifully and made sure her big sister was set and ready for the big day, looking beautiful and stunning. As Desmarie goes to hug her, Ruth comes up to them to share the group hug. So warm, so happy, Desmarie was glad to have her family together with her on this special day.

Desmarie and Desmonte walk into the room where the service was going to be held. Their entire family, from both sides, enter the room right behind them and stand by as Desmonte and Desmarie get married. Applause begins to roar with cheering as Desmonte and Desmarie say "I do" and kiss. The rings on their hands never looked so good on anyone else's hands. Since the wedding ceremony was small, Desmonte made sure to make the reception a bigger deal. The couple led their family to Texas de Brazil, a super yummy Brazilian steakhouse restaurant that was located by the mall next to the hotel. Having gone to eat at that restaurant multiple times before, Desmonte and Desmarie knew that their families would love it, and indeed they all did. They had their own private dining room in the back area, where waiters brought out huge skewers of meat and cut them at the table in front of them. Sides and beverages were also accompanied together with the meats. It ended up being such a fun and truly amazing experience to share with everyone. Desmarie felt her best and ate so much meat next to Desmonte. Both families spent the rest of the remaining hours of the evening reservation talking to everyone and taking pictures of the wedding day celebration.

Desmarie's family headed back to New Jersey that week, but promised to come back and visit about a week after Desmarie delivers the baby to help the couple out at home. Already knowing that it would be a tough new transition, speaking of it the greatest way possible, Ruth made sure that she and Lilly would make it back to Florida around the beginning of January; since Desmarie's due date was set to be on Christmas Eve.

CHAPTER 29

Welcome to the World, My Baby Girl

Coming to the end of her pregnancy that year, her incredible and successful baby shower that was celebrated at her father in-law's home in October sparked some good memories now. Desmarie and Desmonte were getting ready to pack their overnight bags for the hospital, it was presently one week before her due date. That same week, they both went to her OB appointments for a check in fluids, vitals and the last ultrasound. Desmarie began to feel uncomfortable as the baby was getting bigger inside of her during the month of December. Sacrificing not drinking wine nor shellfish, not being able to eat soft cheeses and cold-cuts for sandwiches, Desmarie was very much looking forward to the delivery date but she was also feeling a little scared. Desmonte made sure to comfort her and reassure her that it was all good. Her sister Patty gave birth to her 3rd son earlier at the end of November with the same doctor. She as well encouraged and sympathized with Desmarie, making sure to also push breastfeeding on her the moment her daughter is born and held in her arms. Yes, it is a girl! Desmarie and Desmonte are about to have a daughter!

The due date came along, Christmas Eve on December 24th. Desmarie and Desmonte were at her sister Patty's house celebrating the holiday with the kids and in-laws. Baby girl inside was cozy and comfortable, and moving slowly but also letting her mom know that she was ok where she was. Desmarie pushed herself to walk some more outside around the complex with Desmonte by her side. The weeks prior, she also did a lot of walking with her sister around the lake nearby. But it looked like her little girl didn't want to come out to the world just yet. Visiting her OB that week, he planned to have a c-section appointment done for Desmarie since: The due date had passed, the baby was already weighed by the final ultrasound to be close to 9lbs, in addition to that her doctor was going on vacation at the end of the month. Desmarie at first didn't accept it, but then thought about it and discussed it with Desmonte. She is at a young age so the recovery shouldn't be too bad. Plus, they could go ahead and make a birth plan right here right now, but if something changes or goes wrong, that plan goes out the window and Desmarie would have to deliver her baby nervously with a doctor that she doesn't even know. With the baby being big in size and possibly making a natural birth difficult to accomplish, in addition to already passing the due date and putting Desmarie at high risk, Desmarie agreed with her doctor and planned the appointment for delivery. Although not crazy about having the surgery, they all felt at the end it was the better option. Desmarie also made sure that while in recovery, to push herself to exercise and move around soon after the surgery while following precautions of course; she wasn't planning to stay on bed rest. The doctor discussed to the couple that recovery would be a piece of cake for Desmarie.

The procedure went well. All of the doctors and nurses at the hospital were great with Desmarie. As she was being prepped for the c-section, one of the assistants in the room placed both of his arms on Desmarie's shoulders to calm her and began to discuss exercises he can do to help his back pain. The conversation helped distract Desmarie, while the other assistant inserted the epidural into Desmarie's lower back. Feeling a burning sensation for a few seconds after, it luckily went away quick and she had no feeling from her waist down. As the nursing staff carried her onto the bed for the procedure, her doctor began cutting in and Desmarie hears Desmonte walk in from the double door. Awaiting to feel something of pain, Desmarie didn't. All she felt was pressure, pretty much like someone was shoving a bunch of water balloons inside her stomach, while someone else was moving them around in the inside. Feeling better and more relaxed, somewhat, Desmarie holds hands with Desmonte as the surgery continued. Everything went pretty smooth, can't complain much. There were, however, two instances where Desmarie felt light-headed, then after felt some nausea but quickly got treated within seconds from the amazing nurses and doctors in the room. Desmarie all of a sudden feels a big weight come off of her as the doctor gets the baby out from the womb. A gentle yet loud cry echoes in the room as the doctor hands the baby to his nurses. Desmonte walks over with the nurse to see his beautiful daughter. He got to help the nurse as she offered him to cut the umbilical cord. Pictures were taken by the staff with Desmonte's phone, especially when the nurse gave the baby to Desmarie for a quick snapshot. Amazing, beautiful, super crazy, and wonderful. This experience was overwhelmingly satisfying and so happy for everyone in the room.

And there you have it, a beautiful baby girl. A three day stay in the hospital, Desmarie began breastfeeding her baby girl day 1. "How does it feel baby, are you doing ok?" Desmonte checks on Desmarie as she holds their daughter in her arms in a football position to not interfere with the incision on her stomach. "I am ok baby, in a little bit of pain but the medicine is kicking in. This really feels amazing, weird but so wonderful," Desmarie describes to him as the baby continues to eat. The feeling is indescribable. Holding her daughter close and to her heart, her touch heals all. Desmonte continues to stare at both of them intently, assuring that they were still ok. He then continued to caress his daughter's small head as she fed on mom's breasts. Life is truly so amazingly incredible.

The first night was the hardest. Getting almost no sleep herself, Desmarie continued feeling so tired. Once she began to finally doze off after the pain went away, one of the nurses would come in to check her vitals and make sure the surgical incision was healing well. "Ok, I need to press down on your stomach to make sure your uterus is shrinking back down to the correct size," the nurse explained to Desmarie. What in the actual fuck did she just say? Oh my god, this is going to hurt. Desmarie kept thinking in her mind about the pain, then turned her head to give a worried look to Desmonte. Desmonte grabbed her hand tight. this was the worst part of the whole thing to be quite honest. "AH OUCH!", Desmarie moaned loudly with pain as the nurse checks her abdomen; pressing down where her incision was. In about 5-6 torturous seconds later, it was over. Desmarie can catch her breath, while Desmonte wipes the sweat off her forehead. Even though Desmarie had a c-section, there was still blood afterwards. So much like a heavy menstrual cycle, to the point where Desmarie had to wear a mesh, pantyhose-like underwear during her stay at the hospital post-partum. Not looking so sexy nor physically attractive, she didn't have to feel self-conscious around her husband who accepts her in whichever way she was.

The day before leaving, Desmarie felt a monumental feat. She accomplished going number 2! After a c-section, she was given prune juice to drink daily and sometimes more than one during the day to hopefully ease a bowel movement out before discharge day. Not being able to push was the hard part, however, Desmarie luckily did it. She felt like a labor warrior. The couple felt like the entire experience was a giant achievement. Not to mention, they got something beautiful out of the whole experience.

The last night spent at the hospital, Desmarie's eyes were heavy and were beginning to close for a quick nap; hopefully. One of the nurses knocked on the door about 10 minutes after falling asleep to check Desmarie's vitals. Glimpsing at the nurse with big her big and light purple eye lids, Desmarie smiled at the nurse and thanked her as she walked out the door. Desmonte was able to luckily stay asleep, while their baby moved a little in her swaddle blanket. Desmarie grinned at her and began to recollect one of the days before she got pregnant. She remembered talking with Desmonte on the couch while the TV was on. It was airing the Amazing Race on the CBS channel. Desmonte looked over to Desmarie and said, "You know that's something we can do with no problem." Desmarie glanced at him in surprise, "Really?

Oh my god that would be so much fun to do! And we can have our kids at home with your mom watching us on TV and cheering us on!" Desmarie had told him excitedly. Desmarie thinks to herself that this has more of a possibility now to come true since they both officially have a daughter now.

CHAPTER 30

Misdirection

Desmonte and Desmarie's daughter was growing each and every day, becoming more beautiful each minute that passed by. From learning how to sit up, stand and walk, her parents fell in love with every milestone that she went through and accomplished. With the huge blessing of having Desmarie's family from New Jersey come down to help on the 2nd week of bringing their beautiful baby home, the couple was extremely grateful to have all of the guidance they can get. It was also great for Desmarie to experience the adventures of her pregnancy with her sister Patty; those 9 months definitely brought them closer together.

Yet to come are the never-ending adventures of life. Enjoy the ride because there is only one. The roads might have bumps and curbs, but with enough force, it can be passed and overcome. How you overcome it, that might also be tricky and injuries might come along the way. But what matters is that you got through it. Look for the light at the end of the tunnel.

If the readers of this book had the possibility to meet the main character of this book, whose name is Desmarie, she would share this with all of you. I would tell you to hold on to that resilience, it will be worth it. Despite of all of the bruises, aches and pains from the past, I promise that you become a much stronger person. Oh yeah, Desmarie is actually me, the author of this book. Hello! Nice to meet all of you. I want to thank you for purchasing my book and taking the time to read all of the chapters from my life. This story was my life growing up from ages 5-27. I am 29 years old now, and super grateful for everything that has happened to me. If you are reading my book now, we have been going through some tough times together. With this worldwide pandemic currently present, it hasn't been easy on any of us. I was unemployed for half the year; I never experienced that ever. Being at home though was actually great because I got to spend it with my husband and daughter safe at home. I felt like I was making up lost time in between, not to mention being there for my two-year old daughter and teaching her the things she did not know yet, such as the ABCs and numbers 1-20.

Writing this book was genuinely my big and long-awaited project for years now. I took advantage and began to work on it during my free time off. I also have to give thanks to my family and friends who pushed me to complete this already. Throughout the years, I was blessed with many compliments about my writing skill, so I finally went ahead and did it.

Listen to the people that love you. They do care about you, trust me. The fault is in us because we as humans make it so damn hard for each other to know what we want. Let your voice be heard, don't be afraid to express how you feel. Communication is key. If you need help, cry out for help, you will be ok if you make it visible to at least one loved one close to you.

Life can be hard. Actually, let me re-word that, life IS hard. But you will get to where you need to be, just trust the timing. The year 2020 has been truly upsetting for the world, and has brought me to feel so much anxiety deep down. I don't want to make this political so I won't. However, I would like to express this: please be kind to others. You don't know the struggles that people are going through. Anger has been amplified this year. Keep in mind that when hatred is loud from someone that people look up to for their own reason, those same individuals and others tend to follow in that example. Listen to perspectives from the community and look for common ground to recognize that reasonable and good people can reach different conclusions. We don't have to change people's minds, just respect them. I used to think differently when I was younger, but now I have changed my views based on everything I've seen and learned from the past decade. I try to look for the good in bad situations, I do that in general with any open discussions and disagreements that come into play. This virus has truly exposed this beautiful country's guards and weaknesses. Let's all work together to make our stomping ground a fair and happy homestead so that others can see what true leaders we are; let's not let anyone change that about us.

Also, when you are making your voice be heard for any reason, remember that everyone is still healing from things they don't speak about aloud. Be patient because healing takes time. Look at what happened to me, I went through shit when I was younger. I try to thank God daily and express my gratitude to my family from New Jersey and husband for saving my life. At one point in the past I chose to almost end my life but decided not to at the end. I still do miss my mom as much as I did in 2002; it will always feel fresh and I will always miss her dearly. She left too soon and that is for sure. It's crazy to think that at my age now, I only had 11 years with her. I've lived more life without her. Missing a mom doesn't go away. But at least the feeling of "I can't go on" went away many years ago thankfully with the love, help, and guidance of my close family and friends. I will mention it again and please don't any of you be ashamed to read this: Blood is NOT thicker than water. Read it, understand it, and believe it, because it is the truth.

Thanks to Lilly, I am who I am now. Growing up and going to school together with her really changed me for the better. From the awkwardly shy young and insecure girl I used to be, she fixed that. Thank you, sis, for showing me that life was worth to continue living, that there was also so much more to learn, explore and discover in the world. Thank you for keeping me sane.

Of course, saving the best for last. To my husband Desmonte, thank you baby for always being here for me. Always being my biggest support, my true love who has made me and continue making me the happiest woman in the world. I really thought my heart would not be filled again with the missing pieces that broke off years ago, but you did it. You filled all of it somehow to be more firm and stronger. You continue to add on to my happiness each and every day, from the moment you open your eyes and look at me each morning. I love you with all of my heart baby, thank you for being with me and accepting all of me.

March 18th, 2017 - The last night in Rome